THE ENGLISHMAN'S HOME

FROM COTTAGE TO CASTLE

The possession of an entire house is strongly desired by every Englishman, for it throws a sharp, well defined circle around his family and hearth – the shrine of his sorrows, joys and meditations.

1851 CENSUS

CONGLETON – *Moreton Old Hall, 1902* 48670

THE ENGLISHMAN'S HOME

FROM COTTAGE TO CASTLE

WITH PHOTOGRAPHS FROM THE FRANCIS FRITH COLLECTION

Compiled and edited by Terence and Eliza Sackett

First published in the United Kingdom in 2006 by The Francis Frith Collection

Hardback Edition ISBN 1-84589-278-X

British Library Cataloguing in Publication Data

The Englishman's Home
Compiled and edited by Terence and Eliza Sackett

The Francis Frith Collection
Frith's Barn, Teffont,
Salisbury, Wiltshire SP3 5QP
Tel: +44 (0) 1722 716 376
Email: info@francisfrith.co.uk
www.francisfrith.com

Designed and assembled by Terence Sackett
Image enhancing by Sue Molloy

Printed in Singapore by Imago

Front Cover: Ringwood, The Millstream 1900 *45027t*

The colour-tinting in this book is for illustrative purposes only, and is not intended to be historically accurate.

CONTENTS

6   Introduction

8   The South-West

38   The South Country

58   Around London and the
     Thames Valley

76   The Western Counties
     and the Welsh Borders

90   The Midlands

102   East Anglia

122   The North

156   Index

158   Francis Frith - Victorian Pioneer

159   Voucher for a free print

INTRODUCTION

THIS BOOK is a celebration of the English house in all its extraordinary diversity.

In it are pictured humble cottages, farmhouses, town houses, urbane terraces and crescents, rectories, country mansions, castles, and a number of unusual and eccentric dwellings. It is a unique survey, in that the period photographs, specially selected from the world-famous Francis Frith Collection, show our English homes as they were before modern 'restoration' altered them for ever. The Frith historical scenes reveal our cottages and houses as they once looked, and probably as their architects intended them to be seen: there are no disfiguring replacement windows or extensions, little jarring modern infill, and most important of all, no obscuring lines of parked cars.

And because we are able to see the streets in their entirety, we are able to gain an understanding of how the individual buildings relate to each other and to the surrounding village or townscape. We will find several fascinating examples, for instance, of how the various local styles and periods rub up against each other – Tudor with Georgian, 18th-century with medieval. In most cases the result is a happy coherence.

The situation is very different from the way our towns and villages look now. Today, if we were blindfolded, and set down at some unknown point in the middle of a town or a new housing estate, it would be nigh

on impossible to say exactly where we are. The houses themselves would give us few clues, for most would be of the type that could be found anywhere in the country – modern communications have made building a nationwide enterprise, and bricks manufactured in Hull, for instance, are often transported all the way to building sites in South Devon. Wherever we are, it is hard to identify any truly contemporary local vernacular. What we find, in general, is a polyglot style, an often unsatisfactory and inconsidered confusion of disparate elements and periods.

Until the 19th century, however, builders invariably lived where they worked, and relied on materials that they could find within a comfortable travelling distance for a horse and cart. They were obliged to make the best of what they had, employing inherited skills and considerable ingenuity. As a result local and regional styles evolved down the centuries, differing widely across the country. In the south-west there was much cob (earth) building and thatch. Timber-framing with lath and plaster or brick infill prevailed in forested areas such as Kent and the Midlands. In places where there was local stone it was vigorously quarried, and for lesser dwellings rubble was collected from nearby fields. For the plainest cottages uneven blocks of stone were used uncoursed, but where a householder was prepared to pay for a more prestigious finish, the stones were cut and dressed into ashlar blocks and then laid in neat courses. In regions where stone was at a premium, bricks were fired using local clays, and because clays and firing conditions varied, a broad range of bricks of pleasing hues of reds and browns resulted, each adding to an area's unique architectural character. Materials were often combined, such as brick and banded flint in Wiltshire and Hampshire. All these building styles and methods could be successfully scaled up and down from the grandest to the most humble, and there are, for instance, timber-framed houses pictured in this book that are grand mansions in their own right, and masterpieces of the joiner's art. Because local materials were used, buildings built at different times and in different styles managed to retain a pleasing harmony.

None of these restraints, of course, applied to the rich, who could do exactly as they wished. They imported raw materials from all over the country, engaged the most prestigious British or European architects, and built extravaganzas that bore no relation to prevailing local styles or conditions – a mock Rhenish castle, a French chateau, a Jacobean-inspired fantasy or a miniature Crystal Palace. Some of our oldest country houses started their lives as defensive castles, and then, as the threat of continual war declined, were gradually converted into luxurious and often palatial mansions fit for dukes and royalty.

Things altered significantly – but fortunately not for the worse – in the 18th century, when the Georgians introduced a uniform, classical style of building that was suitable for both town and country. Dignified and urbane, it formed the magnificent terraces of Bath and Cheltenham as well as the humblest cottages we find in villages all over the country. It was a masterpiece of unification, and has created a rich and lasting legacy for architects to draw on ever since.

What we see on the surface of buildings is not always the whole story. This book reveals how houses, grand and humble, have been continually remodelled down the centuries as fashions changed. Indeed, it is often very

difficult to precisely date a building from its outward appearance – we see here plaster concealing primitive cruck timbers, or a smart Georgian stone frontage disguising an earlier humble timber or cob wall; we see roofs raised, windows altered or added, and wings attached, as prevailing styles or the social status of the owners fluctuated.

There is also in England a rich heritage of unusal and eccentric dwellings, used by both rich and poor. We see in this book many ingenious and curious housing solutions – a gypsy caravan (a 19th-century phenomenon); caves turned into dwellings; a converted fishing smack and a narrow boat; folly towers and a disguised water-tower; a converted watermill and windmill; and a chalet bungalow.

Everything changed with the onslaught of industrial manufacture in the 19th century. Country people emigrated into the towns in search of work, and speculative builders were soon running up entire neighbourhoods of terraced houses, all built from uniform industrially manufactured bricks. It was the beginning of the end for local distinctiveness.

This book offers us a unique perspective of English vernacular architecture. The quotations from celebrated writers, poets and travellers down the centuries add to the authentic atmosphere. They offer us impressions of how our towns and villages were viewed by previous ages and generations. Invariably vividly written, they are often unexpectedly outspoken.

This pictorial survey should leave every one of us astonished at the sheer wealth of our surviving building heritage. Let us hope it encourages us to continue to protect our historic buildings now and into the future.

Opposite: SMALLHYTHE, ELLEN TERRY'S HOUSE C1955 S701070
Above: BROUGHTON CASTLE 1922 72110
Left: RAMSBURY, BURDETT STREET 1906 57200

POLPERRO – *Sturdy fishermen's houses built on the solid rock*

THE SHELL HOUSE, according to a guided walk leaflet, 'was decorated by a retired naval man in the 1950s using his lifetime's collection from around the world'. At the time of this photograph, the Shell House was called Peacehaven; a sign on the steps put up by the concerned owner asks plaintively: 'Please do not handle the shells'. Eccentric and exuberant, this amusing kind of decoration can be found in other seaside villages too. The street in which the Shell House stands is The Warren, its name reflecting the fact that this area was used in medieval times for farming rabbits for meat.

POLPERRO nestles comfortably inside the slate ledges and cliffs of a narrow inlet. Stone-built, whitewashed cottages huddle around the water's edge. These cottages, many slate-hung and with outside stone staircases, seem to grow out of the very rock, and the town has been poetically described as 'a human bees' nest stowed away in a cranny of the rocks'. This cottage was once an infamous refuge for smugglers and a store house for their contraband.

Above:
POLPERRO, THE SHELL HOUSE C1955   P68133
Left:
POLPERRO, AN OLD SMUGGLER'S COTTAGE
1924   76344P

ST IVES – *A labyrinth of courtyards and cottages, set between a broad beach and a fishing harbour*

DOWNALONG, or Down'long in its popular form, is the name used for old St Ives at its most authentic by born and bred St Ives people. Down'long is defined roughly as the area of granite cottages, houses and other buildings that surrounds the harbour and straddles the neck of land between the high promontory of the Island and the inland parts of the town. Within this area lie numerous streets and alleyways that wriggle to and fro like granite canyons between the buildings, such as the Digey, Teetotal Street, Love Lane, Virgin Street and Mount Zion. They lead to the Island, and to Barnoon, a higher part of the old town above Porthmeor Beach. Around the Digey area is where the town's oldest buildings survive and where the real flavour of St Ives can be enjoyed. In numerous courtyards and open-sided cellars, where flowers blossom amidst colourful paintwork and golden granite, pilchards and herring were once laid out or 'baulked' into carefully arranged piles. Here we see a row of typical fishermen's cottages with steps up to the front door and storage for fishing paraphernalia below.

Above: ST IVES, BETHESDA HILL 1890 24185
Right: ST IVES, BACK ROAD EAST 1906 56548

The houses are closely packed, or rather jumbled together with the narrowest and crookedest streets and courts in which to get about or up and down. They have a look of individuality, like a crowd of big rough men pushing and elbowing one another for room, and you can see how this haphazard condition has come about when you stumble by chance on a huge mass of rock thrusting up out of the earth among the houses. There was, in fact, just this little sheltered depression in a stony place to build upon, and the first settlers, no doubt, set their houses just where and how they could among the rocks, and when more room was wanted more rocks were broken down and other houses added until the town as we find it resulted. It is all rude and irregular, as if produced by chance or nature, and altogether reminds one of a rabbit warren or the interior of an ants' nest.

W H HUDSON, 'THE LAND'S END', 1908

PORTHCURNO – *House and beach hut set in a deep cliff crevice*

NOW RUINOUS, this curious little house was built into a crevice in the granite cliff on the west side of Porthcurno beach. It was used as an up-market beach hut in the 1930s by Rowena Cade while she was making her open air theatre just above – a poster on the door appears to be advertising a play at the Minack Theatre.

THE ISLES OF SCILLY – *a primitive thatched stone shelter*

THIS LOVELY PICTURE of an old cottage on the Isles of Scilly was probably taken in Old Town. The cottage is built from huge blocks of roughly shaped stone set in irregular courses. The sash windows at the front are relatively sophisticated for a cottage of this type. The thatch is sewn to the rafters by criss-cross ropes to withstand the gales. Thatch in the Scillies was usually straw, or sometimes bracken. The woman smiles toward her husband and child by the front door. The little girl stands proudly in her Sunday best.

Above right: PORTHCURNO,
THE HOUSE IN THE ROCKS C1955   P81014

Above left: PORTHCURNO 1908   61259

Left: ST MARY'S, THE ISLES OF SCILLY,
AN OLD COTTAGE 1892   31128A

PRIDEAUX PLACE was built above the church, possibly on the site of the original monastery. Later it became the site of a grange farm and tithe barn belonging to Bodmin Priory. In anticipation of the Dissolution of the Monasteries by Henry VIII, Humphrey and Nicholas Prideaux advised the priory to lease their lands and properties to friends at nominal rents. Humphrey Prideaux's son married the prior's niece, and they were given a 99-year lease on the Manor of Padstow as a wedding present. The Prideauxs took over as lords of the manor of Padstow from the priors of Bodmin, and Prideaux Place became the manor house.

Another Nicholas Prideaux rebuilt the house between 1581 and 1592 in the fashionable E-shape of the age. The house underwent considerable alteration in the 18th and 19th centuries, but the front remained largely unaltered. Parts became derelict, and today only 6 of its 46 bedrooms are habitable. Some remain exactly as the American Army left them before D-Day in the Second World War.

The house was built in an elevated position and is surrounded by trees. Trees and parkland are rare in north Cornwall because of the prevailing westerly winds, and the trees here form a shelter belt for the house and gardens. The gardens used to be open to the public only for special events, but in recent years they have been regularly opening in the summer months. Interest has arisen since Prideaux Place featured in films and TV series, including 'Twelfth Night' and 'Coming Home'.

PADSTOW – *Prideaux Place, grand house with monastic origins*

In the Elizabethan house the Oak Room (below) was the Great Hall. Tudor panelling depicts carved female figures, one of which is supposed to be Elizabeth I. Their arms are articulated, and during the Civil War they were said to be raised or lowered at dinner parties to indicate whether there were sympathisers of the opposite side present. Edmund Prideaux remodelled the room in the 18th century, and much of the panelling dates from this time. Restored after a fire in the 1890s, the room still retains its function as a dining room. The dining chairs are by Augustus Pugin, architect of the House of Commons and leader of the Gothic revival. The picture over the fireplace is of Nicholas Prideaux by Marcus Gheeraerts the Younger, and is similar to his portrait of Sir Francis Drake. The ruff collar was added when Nicholas was knighted.

There is much else to see at Prideaux Place. The decorations in the Grenville Room came from Sir Richard Grenville's manor at Stowe in north Cornwall. The fittings include a mirror surround carved by Grinling Gibbons, and many interesting paintings. In the morning room there are several portraits by the 18th-century Cornish artist John Opie.

Above:
PADSTOW,
PRIDEAUX PLACE
1903 49951

Right: PADSTOW,
PRIDEAUX PLACE,
THE OAK ROOM
1888 21204

NEWQUAY – *The huer's house: from here he watched for the shoals of pilchard far out in the bay*

THE HUER'S HOUSE is identical today, even down to the granite railing posts. Sited up on the headland near the harbour, this is where the huer, who had to have very good eyesight, waited to spot the purple stain on the sea that heralded an incoming pilchard shoal.

He would raise the alarm by crying 'hevva! hevva!' ('here they are!') through his trumpet, or loud hailer, and would use signals made with two 'bushes' (originally gorse bushes) to direct the fishing fleet to the shoal out in the bay. The steps on the outside of the hut gave the huer an even better vantage point. Wilkie Collins, the 19th-century novelist, thought that the huer waving his bushes would resemble 'a maniac of the most dangerous character' to an outsider. The huer was paid a guinea a week, and also a percentage of the value of the fish taken. The hut offered rather basic accommodation for the huer, who would take up his post several days before the shoals of pilchard were expected. Here he would live during the hours of daylight for up to four months of the year. The 'hue and cry' was an exciting sound for the whole fishing community, and many traditional rhymes reflect that:

> *THE PILCHARDS are come, and hevva is heard,*
> *And the town from the top to the bottom is stirred.*
> *Anxious faces are hurrying in every direction.*
> *To take a fine shoal they have no objection …*
> *We see the huer with bushes in hand*
> *Upon the white rock he now takes his stand.*
> *While 'Right off,' 'Win tow boat,' 'Hurray' and 'Cowl rooze'*
> *Are signals no seiner will ever refuse.*

Above: NEWQUAY, THE HUER'S HOUSE 1907 59333
Below: BOSCASTLE, THE VILLAGE 1906 56170

BOSCASTLE – *A sturdy granite cottage*

THE RUGGED harbour of Boscastle is an important, if unreliable, haven for shipping on this treacherous coast. The old rhyme reminds us of the constant danger here: 'From Padstow Point to Lundy Light, Is a sailor's grave by day or night'. At Boscastle, a romantic-looking inlet twists and turns for half a mile between brooding cliffs of slate and shale. The sea churns constantly, and the cove offers little protection for vessels berthing at the diminutive pier. Hawsers 'thick as a man's thigh' check the impetus of boats entering on the tide. From the harbour, a long, picturesque street of granite cottages climbs uphill. Houses like Vulcan House, seen here, were built as fortresses against the Atlantic storms. Thick rubble walls and huge porches kept the weather out, and tall sturdy chimneys testify to blazing fireplaces inside.

Down here the building stone is either granite or elvan; and rough-cast is desirable, as both sorts take damp, especially the granite. If the walls are built of unsquared stone, the rain will sometimes find its way between the joints and down into the wall, wherever the bedding of the stones slopes downwards from the outside … Some of the older buildings have squared stones from three to five feet long and two or three feet high. But generally these do not go beyond the first few courses, and then comes unsquared stone, and very often cob on top. In most of the old buildings here the walls are constructed with an inner and an outer face of unsquared stone and a core of rubble between – the walls are seldom less than three feet thick – and when the mortar has decayed, there is nothing to keep the outside stones from falling off and the rubble going after them; and then the whole structure may come tumbling down.

CECIL TORR, 'SMALL TALK AT WREYLAND', 1926

LUSTLEIGH *– Wreyland, Cecil Torr's peaceful paradise*

LUSTLEIGH VILLAGE, on the edge of Dartmoor, is still a showpiece of the thatcher's art. West Country thatching is done with straw, rather than the reed that is used in other parts of the country, but the tools are much the same – iron hooks, hand shears, shearing hook, sparhook and leggat.

Wreyland is an ancient settlement a little along from the village. This house, probably 16th- or 17th-century, is typical of those found on the eastern side of Dartmoor. Its walls are hidden beneath some rather weathered rendering, but are almost certainly made of granite, which can be seen in the arch below the gable, and in the horse trough in which the little boy is standing. The historian and diarist Cecil Torr lived here for most of his life during the late 19th and early 20th centuries.

Above: LUSTLEIGH, WREYLAND 1906 56595P

GALMPTON – *Traditional Devon cob and thatch*

'All that cob needs is a good hat and a good pair of shoes'.

IF COB gets damp, it crumbles; what it needs is a good protection of thatch and a stone foundation. Cob was an unsophisticated way to build. Labourers about to be married would begin on their cottages and work leisurely at them so that they were ready for their new bride. Thomas Hardy described the process:

What was called mud-wall was really a composition of chalk, clay and straw – essentially unbaked brick. This was mixed up into a sort of dough-pudding close to where the cottage was to be built. The mixing was performed by treading and shovelling – women sometimes being called in to tread – and the straw was added to bind the mass together … It was then thrown by pitchforks on to the wall, where it was trodden down to a thickness of about two feet, till a rise of about three feet had been reached. This was left to settle for a day or two [and then another layer was added].

THOMAS HARDY, FROM A LETTER TO THE TIMES, 11 MARCH 1927

WEST BUCKLAND is a remote hamlet a little to the east of Bantham in the South Hams. Just behind the small boy is Tidley Cottage, built of cob in the 17th century. Its long straw thatch is laid flat (unlike thatch made from reeds) and firmly pegged down. This cottage was one of the smallest in Devon, measuring just 15ft by 10ft 9in. The occupants had to climb a ladder to reach the tiny bedroom through the window; upstairs they had to bend, for there was no room to stand up. Tidley Cottage burned down in 1959, and the site is now taken by a garage.

Opposite left: GALMPTON, THE VILLAGE 1927 79897
Above left: THATCHERS AT WORK IN PORLOCK, SOMERSET C1950 P74043
Below left: WEST BUCKLAND, NEAR THURLESTONE, THE VILLAGE 1920 69843

WEST BUCKLAND – *Cob and thatch in miniature*

HOPE COVE
– A safe refuge from the sea

HOPE COVE lies on Bigbury Bay in the shelter of Bolt Tail. It used to be a simple fishing village cut off from the world; the villagers fished for pilchards and mackerel, and supplemented their income by plundering wrecked ships – and by smuggling.

The village is in fact two villages, Outer Hope and Inner Hope; at Inner Hope, cob and stone cottages cluster around a tiny square. Today, the fishing has declined, although crabs and lobsters are still caught here; many of the picturesque cottages are holiday homes. In this photograph, cottagers are at their doors, and canaries sing from cages on each side of the porch. A charming cobbled path meanders along the row.

Above: HOPE COVE, COTTAGES 1890 25260

TORQUAY – *Compton Castle, a fortified manor house in a lush Devon combe*

DESPITE its name, this is actually a fortified manor house, built in the 14th to 16th centuries by the Gilbert family and one of the few fortified houses in Britain to survive without later alterations or additions. Here we see it in some disrepair, but it was restored in the 20th century and presented to the National Trust. The completed defences (including a twenty-foot-high curtain wall) could withstand an attack from a roving shore party, and the castle's location, hidden in a lush South Devon combe, was an added safeguard against surprise attack. In 1800 the estate was sold by the Gilbert family, and for the next century the building was neglected; but in 1930 Commander Walter Raleigh Gilbert, 11th in line from Sir Humphrey Gilbert, bought back the property. Commander and Mrs Gilbert meticulously restored the house and rebuilt the great hall, which had become ruinous in the 18th century. Their restoration work was completed by them after the National Trust were given the property in 1951.

Left: TORQUAY, COMPTON CASTLE 1890 25936

TORQUAY – *Elegant seaside terraces, built by landowner Robert Cary for Victorian visitors to Torbay*

Above: TORQUAY, ABBEY CRESCENT 1896   38598

DURING the first decades of Victoria's long reign Torquay enjoyed the epithet 'Queen of Watering Places', as most of her visitors were, as one account put it, 'of the highest class'. Just before this photograph was taken, the emphasis on encouraging invalids to come to Torquay was at its height. One guidebook reported: 'This watering place … is much resorted to by invalids with delicate lungs … The general effect of the white houses, the grey limestone cliffs, and the foliage and greensward … is unusually pleasant and picturesque, and calculated to soothe, as far as scenery can soothe, the lassitude and depression of ill-health'. Soon afterwards, in 1892, through trains came to Torquay, and the town became a holiday resort as opposed to a retreat for invalids. Torquay's development is due to the two main landowners of the time, Sir Laurence Palk (on whose behalf town plans were drawn up in 1805) and Robert Cary. This elegant terrace, built in the late 1850s, was Mr Cary's creation, which attempted to emulate the grander efforts – The Terrace, Hesketh Crescent, and Lisburne Crescent – of Sir Laurence. It has an ornamental centre, matching bays and end pediments. It is little changed at the date of this photograph since it was built in the late 1850s.

SIDMOUTH – *A plain farmhouse is converted to a charming Regency pastiche of Gothic*

IT WAS around 1700 that the Royal Glen was built by a Mr King of Bath. It was then a modest farmhouse with a dairy, outhouses, a hayloft and a well that still exists in the centre of the house. It was first known as King's Cottage, taking the name of the owner. In 1775 the house was part of the manor estates. When in 1817 it was purchased by Major General Edward Baynes, he added considerably to the grounds, made several general improvements, and changed the name to Woolbrook Cottage; it was sometimes known as Woolbrook Glen. The house was converted from a farmhouse into Regency splendour with delightful castellated pediments, a tent-roofed veranda, and Gothic casements complete with painted drip moulds. The inside was as charming, especially the elegant and graceful drawing room. The house has a regal presence; today the royal coat of arms is proudly depicted on the plaque above the Gothicised porch.

EXMOUTH
– A unique 16-sided house

THIS MOST UNUSUAL house, now owned by the National Trust, is situated two miles from the centre of Exmouth. A La Ronde was built in 1795 by eccentric spinster cousins, Jane and Mary Parminter, after their 10-year Grand Tour of Europe; one architectural influence is said to be the Byzantine-style Basilica of San Vitale in Ravenna. A La Ronde still contains many of its original contents, which include collections and souvenirs assembled by the Parminters on their travels. The 16-sided house was designed to catch maximum sunlight; the cousins could follow the sun round the house during the course of the day - the lofty central octagonal hall has eight doors leading to interconnecting rooms. There is a shell-encrusted gallery and staircase now so fragile that they can only be viewed on closed-circuit television. In the early 19th century, Exmouth was a highly fashionable resort: residents included Lady Byron and Viscountess Nelson.

THIS CHARMING cottage orné, with its neat thatch, Gothic windows and pretty veranda, is another example of Sidmouth's quirky Regency architecture.

Above: SIDMOUTH, AN OLD COTTAGE 1907   58054

Opposite: SIDMOUTH, THE ROYAL GLEN HOTEL C1955   S129052P

Above: EXMOUTH, A LA RONDE 1906   53960

CLOVELLY – *A medley of cottages of all shapes and sizes cling to the steep cobbled path leading down to the harbour*

CLOVELLY'S remarkable state of preservation is due to the philanthropic nature of the Hamlyn family, who acquired the manor in 1740. Christine Hamlyn took charge of things in 1886 and founded the Clovelly Estate Company, which runs the village to this day. Donkeys were used to transport everything up and down Clovelly's steep street: herring, coal and lime came up the hill from the harbour. The only safe anchorage on the inhospitable, craggy coastline between Appledore and Boscastle, Clovelly lived precariously for centuries from the herring fishery.

However, Charles Kingsley's use of the village as a location in 'Westward Ho!' alerted the new breed of holidaymaker to the charm of its steep, cobbled streets; by 1890 there were three hotels. Clovelly grew organically. The houses were built (mostly of cob) by the fishermen as and when they were needed, and thanks to the precipitous setting, display a remarkable variety of sizes, shapes and styles which somehow manage to harmonise perfectly together.

Above: CLOVELLY, THE STREET 1908 61005P

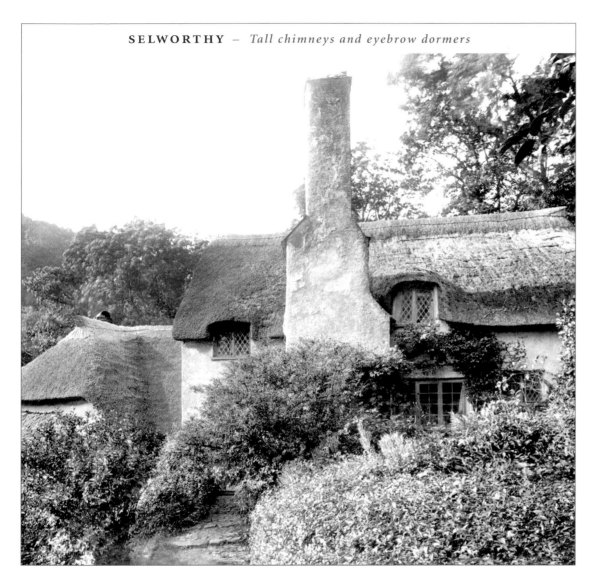

SELWORTHY – *Tall chimneys and eyebrow dormers*

THE VILLAGE of Selworthy is part of the Holnicote Estate, the gift of the Acland family to the National Trust, to which many of the village's thatched cottages now belong – their preservation is thus assured. Below is a romantic but perceptive description of thatch and its gradual weathering by R Boswell Smith.

It was once believed that Sir Thomas Acland built Selworthy's cottages in 1828, but it has recently been discovered that they were adapted from medieval farmhouses already standing. At one time, the external walls of many of the cottages in the area were coated with a weatherproofing mixture of lime and tallow, but only at Selworthy is this practice maintained. Semi-circular ovens protrude from the walls beside the chimneys on a few of these cottages. They were used to bake bread, then as always a diet staple.

Left: SELWORTHY,
THE ALMSHOUSES 1900   45701

Notice the exquisitely neat finish of the roof-ridge, the most critical point of the whole: the geometrical patterns formed by the spars just below, which help, by their grip, to hold it in its place for years: the faultless symmetry of the slopes, the clean-cut edges, the gentle curves of the upper windows which rise above the 'plate'; and, better still, the embrace which, as with the encircling arms of a mother it gives to the deep-planted, half-hidden dormer window in the middle of the roof, nestling lovingly within it, and by its very look inviting to peacefulness and repose. Note, too, the change of colouring in the work as time goes on; the rich sunset tint, beautiful as the locks of Ceres, when the work is just completed; the warm brown of the succeeding years; the emerald green, the symptom of advancing age, when lichens and moss have begun to gather thick upon it; and 'last scene of all, which ends' its quiet, uneventful history, when winds and rain have done their work upon it, the rounded meandering ridges, and the sinuous deep-cut furrows, which, like the waters of a troubled sea, ruffle its once smooth surface.

R BOSWORTH SMITH, 'THE OLD THATCHED RECTORY', C1880

YEOVIL – *Cottage by the springs*

JUST a short walk from the town centre leads to Nine Springs, one of Yeovil's beauty spots. This ever-popular place was originally a Victorian garden, constructed in the grounds of Aldon House, home to the Batten family. It was designed around springs bubbling from the hillside, which were channelled into a series of waterfalls and ponds. The area of woodland provided a haven of natural beauty and wildlife for the Victorians and Edwardians of Yeovil to enjoy, with footpaths, bridges and waterfalls, and, of course, the nine springs. A network of woodland paths still provides a pleasant stroll. Much of the original planting and design is still in evidence today, although this picturesque cottage with its tumbling thatch and diamond-paned casements, where once afternoon teas were served, is no longer here – it fell into disrepair after the Second World War and was eventually demolished some years later.

Above: YEOVIL, NINE SPRINGS 1912 64531A
Right: GLASTONBURY, THE TRIBUNAL 1886 19009

IN GLASTONBURY'S High Street stands the Tribunal. It dates from the early 15th century, and is so called because it was thought to be the courthouse of the abbots. In fact the first use of the name was as recent as 1791, and the building is now considered to have been built as the house of a wealthy local merchant. The original timber front was replaced with stone around 1500; the emblems over the door are the Tudor rose and the Tudor royal arms. The house was later used by the infamous Judge Jeffreys when he was trying supporters of the Duke of Monmouth after the failure of the Monmouth Rebellion. For a time in the 19th century the Tribunal was a school, but it is now a museum, displaying finds from the Glastonbury lake village. This is an interesting pre-museum photograph, with the building showing signs of dereliction in the windows and roof.

GLASTONBURY – *The Tribunal, the house of a 15th-century merchant*

MONTACUTE – *Montacute House, a glorious composition in warm local Ham Hill stone*

MONTACUTE is a delightful Ham stone-built village, a few miles north of Yeovil. Montacute House (now in the stewardship of the National Trust) lies to the northeast: it is a superb E-plan country house of the 1590s of three storeys, built for the wealthy lawyer Sir Edward Phelips, also in the warm apricot-coloured Ham Hill stone. The splendid façade is virtually a wall of windows and decorative carving. The top windows are those of the 172ft long gallery, stretching from one end of the house to the other, which now contains the Tudor collections of the National Portrait Gallery. When the Powys family lived in the village, the great house was empty, and the children could play in the gallery.

Above: MONTACUTE HOUSE 1900   45333

How the lonely memories of the old gallery would be scattered, as, with the careless voices of living children, we burst in upon its emptiness; and how hollow, how resonant, its bare boards would sound as our quick feet went pattering, racing down them, unheedful of anything but the impinging actuality of our moment's holiday! … The great rocking-horse was kept there, the highest-stepping dapple gray ever built by a carpenter, left alone through so many long hours to contemplate with painted eye the procrastinating twilights of the morning and evening shading their way through sixteen windows, along the coved ceiling of this vast Elizabethan corridor.

LLEWELYN POWYS, 'SOMERSET ESSAYS', BODLEY HEAD, 1937

BATH – *Wood's urbane masterpiece of Georgian terraces and crescents*

The wide, clean ways; the solid, stone-built houses with their dignified aspect; the large distances, terrace beyond terrace; mansions and vast green lawns and parks and gardens; avenues and groups of stately trees, especially the unmatched clump of old planes in the Circus; the whole town, the design in the classic style of one master mind, set by the Avon, amid green hills, produced a sense of harmony and repose which cannot be equalled by any other town in the kingdom.

W H HUDSON, 'AFOOT IN ENGLAND', 1909

BATH is rightly designated a UNESCO World Heritage Site. It is perhaps the most remarkably architecturally unified town in England, a quite outstanding example of Georgian town planning, the vision of a father and son, John Wood the Elder and John Wood the Younger. Their vision was carried on by inspired architects like Thomas Baldwin in the later 18th century. Who can forget the stunning architectural impact of the vast Royal Crescent or the sinuously curving Lansdown Crescent? From about 1720 to the 1820s, a unique and mercifully still complete Georgian city was created. John Wood the Elder built Queen Square in 1728, where he designed each side as 'palace fronts'. This was an idea he probably copied from 1720s terraces in London's Grosvenor Square: the terraced houses, usually three windows or bays wide, are built as if they are a vast palace façade, with a centrepiece, usually pedimented, and the end houses treated as end pavilions. This rapidly became the norm not only in Bath but elsewhere in England, and helped significantly in giving the townscape great dignity and coherence.

Left: BATH, QUEEN SQUARE 1901 46474

ORIGINALLY NAMED King's Circus, the Circus is a complete circle, and was laid out by John Wood the Elder in 1754. Work started in February of that year, but Wood himself died in May, and the work had to be completed by his son, John Wood the Younger. There are three equal and similar blocks, with paired columns flanking each window on each of the three storeys: a Roman circus turned inside out. By the mid 1960s the grime of a coal fire age had to be cleaned off. The central railings were removed during the war to help the munitions industry.

Above: BATH, THE CIRCUS 1911 63686

The Circus has been less favourably received by critics: in Smollett's words, 'it is a pretty bauble, contrived for show, and looks like Vespasian's amphitheatre turned inside out'. One great charm of Bath, especially in the more wealthy parts of the town, is the ample space on which the houses stand and the abundance of trees. The irregularity of the ground also adds to its beauty, and to the labour of walking about the place; for steeper roads than some of the streets offer will not be readily found in an English town.

VICTORIAN GUIDEBOOK C1890

HENBURY – *Blaise Hamlet, Nash's picturesque fantasy*

NINE STORYBOOK thatched cottages at Henbury, each one different, were designed in 1809 by the architect John Nash, the master of the Picturesque style. They are grouped round a village green, and in the centre is a sundial on a stone pillar with a village pump below. The cottages were commissioned by the Quaker banker and philanthropist John Harford to accommodate retired employees of his Blaise Estate. Harford himself lived in Blaise Castle house, built between 1796 and 1798 – the dairy and conservatory were also designed by Nash. The house is set in grounds designed by the landscape gardener Humphrey Repton. Blaise was described by Jane Austen in 'Northanger Abbey' as 'the finest place in England'. These charming houses are still lived in today.

Above: HENBURY, BLAISE HAMLET C1960 H164005

Below: HENBURY, BLAISE HAMLET C1960 H164301

FROME – *The diminutive 'pepper pot'*

AT the south end of Frome's Cheap Street were the premises of H R Hughes; the building, known locally as 'the pepper pot', has a narrow three-sided front and a stone-tiled roof, also with three planes. Advertisements for Grape Nuts, Bovril and Rowntree's Cocoa give a clue to Mr Hughes's stock, sold from what Frith called the oldest house in Frome. To the left, Eagle Lane climbs towards the west end of the Market Place. We must not forget that shops are houses too – small shopkeepers even now still live above their commercial premises.

The building now has a plate glass frontage stretching its entire width, and mock-tudor timbering above. It is a thriving coffeeshop and gallery.

Above: FROME, THE OLDEST HOUSE 1907 58851P

WEYMOUTH – *19th-century seaside exuberance fronting a broad beach and bay*

WEYMOUTH owes its origins as a favourite resort to the patronage of George III and of the rest of fashionable Georgian society, who travelled to the town to take up the new 'cure' of sea bathing. Many of the buildings along the Parade date back to this period. Queen Victoria's reign brought huge changes for the town, which expanded considerably during the 19th century as it attempted to cater for the large increase in tourists. Much building work and renovations were carried out on the seafront properties as they were adapted into lodging houses and hotels. In this photograph we see the Esplanade, with the red brick of Royal Terrace followed by the late Victorian exuberance of the Royal Hotel. Beyond it the terraces stretch on for half a mile – 'Has any coast town a more spectacular seafront than Weymouth?' says Pevsner.

Below: WEYMOUTH, THE ESPLANADE 1899   43852

EYPE – *Edith Warren's teashop*

LOOKING at this lonely stretch of coast near Bridport, with its wild headlands and deserted coves, it is easy to understand why so many local people engaged in smuggling as well as fishing. When this photograph was taken, a number of smugglers were still alive. Eype village ('eype' means 'steep place') is a quarter of a mile inland from the seashore, in a combe below the rolling Dorset downlands. Many of its houses date from the 18th and 19th centuries; little is known of its past history. In this photograph, Edith Warren stands at her door: she augmented her income by offering 'Accommodation for Tea Parties' and ginger beer and lemonade. The thatch looks in need of repair – moss is taking over. By the 1950s, a buttress had been added to the left of the cottage, and also a new window, and the cottage was a general store.

Left: EYPE, JESSAMINE COTTAGE 1897   40089P

THE OLD TOWN of Milton Abbas developed around 10th-century Milton Abbey (behind the photographer). However, in 1780 Joseph Damer (later Lord Milton, 1st Earl of Dorchester) had the town demolished because he disliked its proximity to his great house (built next to the abbey); he employed Capability Brown to erect a new model village half a mile away. Damer moved those inhabitants he could not drive away to the new village, and only one thatched cottage of the old town survives. One stubborn inhabitant refused to move and was flooded out by Mr Damer. The villager later won his case in court. The 'new' village was built all at once in a single sloping street that runs along a steep-sided valley. The identical thatched cob cottages are evenly spaced, each with a garden slanting up behind and grass in front; the effect is both orderly and picturesque. Originally, each cottage housed two families – the single front door led to a common hall – but most of the houses are now single dwellings. In the 19th century they were very overcrowded; it is said that 36 people lived in one of the cottages.

Below:
MILTON ABBAS, THE VILLAGE C1955   M80011

MILTON ABBAS – *A Georgian model village of thatched cottages*

WOOL – *Woolbridge Manor, where Tess spent her honeymoon with Angel Clare*

SET BESIDE the five-arched stone bridge across the River Frome, this 17th-century manor was once the home of the Turberville family, and is immortalised in Thomas Hardy's novel 'Tess of the D'Urbervilles'. On a landing inside this mellow stone and brick building with its three prominent chimneys are the wall paintings which frightened Tess on her honeymoon here with Angel Clare. At the start of the Edwardian period it was still a farmhouse, but it has since become a luxury hotel. The symmetrical and perhaps rather plain entrance front is brought character by the roundels flanking the porch – they 'give the façade just the cachet it needs', says Pevsner.

Above: WOOL, WOOLBRIDGE MANOR 1904   52731

Left: WOOL, WOOLBRIDGE MANOR (AS A HOTEL) C1965   W344072

They drove by the level road along the valley to a distance of a few miles, and, reaching Wellbridge, turned away from the village to the left, and over the great Elizabethan bridge which gives the place half its name. Immediately behind it stood the house wherein they had engaged lodgings, whose exterior features are so well known to all travellers through the Froom Valley; once a portion of a fine manorial residence, and the property and seat of a d'Urberville, but since its partial demolition a farmhouse.

THOMAS HARDY, 'TESS OF THE D'URBERVILLES', 1891

PUDDLETOWN – *rural sophistication*

PUDDLETOWN is rich in associations with Thomas Hardy, for this pleasant and busy village is the Weatherbury of his novel 'Far From the Madding Crowd'. Hardy was a regular visitor, calling on his mother's sisters, Maria and Mary. Though still little larger than a village in the mid 19th century (with 1,330 inhabitants), it thought of itself as a small town. This attractive thatched house dominates the centre of the village. It was built in the early 19th century; its bowed glazed upper bay, the centre part a Venetian window, is supported by slim Tuscan columns. Colourwashed cottages cluster all around.

Right: PUDDLETOWN, THE SQUARE C1966 P163011

THE POET and novelist Thomas Hardy was born in this cottage, a few miles east of Dorchester, on 3 June 1840. It was built by his great-grandfather in 1801, and it is set in the wild country that Hardy called Egdon Heath. He portrayed it as 'a world of shepherds and ploughmen … where modern improvements were still regarded as wonders.' It was from this intensely rural background that he found models for the vividly portrayed characters of his novels. He lived here with his parents and one brother and two sisters. The National Trust now owns the cottage.

*It faces west, and round the back and sides
High beeches, bending, hang a veil of boughs,
And sweep against the roof. Wild honeysucks
Climb on the walls, and seem to sprout a wish
(If we may fancy wish of trees and plants)
To overtop the apple-trees hard by …*

*Our house stood quite alone, and those tall firs
And beeches were not planted. Snakes and efts
Swarmed in the summer days, and nightly bats
Would fly about our bedrooms. Heathcroppers
Lived on the hills, and were our only friends;
So wild it was when we first settled here.*

FROM 'DOMICILIUM', THOMAS HARDY

HIGHER BOCKHAMPTON – *Thomas Hardy's birthplace*

Above: HIGHER BOCKHAMPTON, THOMAS HARDY'S BIRTHPLACE C1955 S771071

WIMBORNE – *A medieval haven of peace: once part of a leper hospital*

A LITTLE OUTSIDE the centre of Wimborne, on the road to Kingston Lacy, stands this charming group of nine cottages and a chapel. In the 13th century, the chapel was part of a leper hospital. In the 17th century, William Stone, who funded the library at Wimborne Minster, endowed the almshouses. This photograph shows one of the oldest of the houses. Behind the photographer more of the almshouses are grouped around a broad area of pretty cottage gardens. The chapel, built in dark brown stone, has a plain, modest interior with bare walls; the paired windows have trefoil tops. The whole complex, beside a now busy road, looks just the same today, and offers visitors an oasis of rest.

Above: WIMBORNE, ST MARGARET'S CHAPEL AND ALMSHOUSES 1908   60634P

CORSHAM – *The Lady Margaret Hungerford almshouses*

CORSHAM STONE is celebrated the world over for its fine grain and quality. The old town buildings, with their steep gables, were built in local stone, creating pleasing and harmonious streets. Many grand buildings in the region are of Corsham stone, including the splendid Lacock Abbey, home of the inventor of photography, Fox Talbot. Corsham Court was built in a local variety called Monk's Park stone. Further afield, Corsham stone can be found in the Royal Exchange and even in Cape Town, where the government buildings incorporate decorative detailing created by masons from this quiet Wiltshire town. One of the architectural treasures of Corsham is the Lady Margaret Hungerford Almshouses and their school. Lady Margaret, widow of Sir Edward Hungerford, founded and endowed the almshouses in 1668 - she was a devout Puritan, and wealthy in her own right. The almshouses originally sheltered six poor people, and this was later increased to a maximum of eight. The school provided free education for ten needy children. Note the baroque pediment and coat-of-arms over the entrance. Two jauntily dressed young men pose for the camera.

Left: CORSHAM, THE ALMSHOUSES 1906   54353P

BIDDESTONE is very much the archetypal English village. Charming stone-built houses, none built later than the early 18th century, are clustered around the green; there are two pubs here too, and the duck pond is host to a wide variety of waterfowl. The 17th-century local grey stone Pool Farmhouse, with the gazebo built into the wall, stands to the centre right. This large handsome house was built in the mid to late 17th century. The local grey stone walls, with flush quoins and moulded copings, are topped with stone-tiled roofs with ball finials on the gables; the delightful gazebo is later, built in the early 18th century in ashlar on a rubble plinth, with a pyramidal roof topped with a ball finial. Its chimney stack indicates that its owners wanted to be prepared for English summers!

BIDDESTONE – *Stone houses around the village green*

Right: BIDDESTONE,
THE VILLAGE C1955   B371002

CASTLE COMBE – *Cotswold charm*

CASTLE COMBE was once a centre for cloth weaving, but it now seems to trade on its picturesque qualities. Indeed, most of the houses in the village, many of them hundreds of years old, are listed so as to preserve the beauty and character of Castle Combe for future generations. The village's favourable microclimate encourages the profusion of climbing plants up the sturdy stone walls of the houses, which have the steep-pitched stone-slated roofs typical of Cotswold villages. The many dormers create a pleasing composition. It must be a strong contender for the 'Prettiest Village in Wiltshire' title. This view gives a good indication of why that should be; the By Brook makes an already attractive scene into something rather special.

Left: CASTLE COMBE, THE VILLAGE 1904   51508P

BUILT BETWEEN 1327 and 1342, the High Street Gate (left) was the main way into Salisbury Cathedral Close. The High Street Gate (sometimes called the North Gate) is still closed every evening, a practice that has continued since about 1340 when the wall surrounding the Close on three sides (the River Avon ran along the other one) was completed. It was built to protect the clergy from the population of the city outside, for in medieval times the church was often unpopular, and the Bishop of Salisbury in particular suffered at the hands of the local mob. The gate housed a night porter and a small gaol. The Close, which provides the physical setting for the cathedral, has survived as well. Built originally to house the clergy, it was begun at the same time as the cathedral itself, and some of the buildings are of the same age. Photograph 56371 shows a typically pleasing mix of houses, some creeper-clad and tile-hung. The architectural heritage that survives in the Close is almost as precious as the cathedral itself. Because of the relatively unchanging pattern of land ownership and use in the Close, even less seems to have altered here over the years. But nowhere escapes completely: more and more vehicular and pedestrian traffic is attracted to the Close each year.

SALISBURY – *Historic cathedral city of Wiltshire, with houses clustered in the Close*

IN a city full of medieval gems, the Hall of John Halle (left) stands out as an extraordinary curiosity. Behind this fake Tudor facade of the late 19th century is a house built 400 years earlier for a wool merchant who became mayor of the city. The Hall is now the entrance foyer of the Odeon Cinema which lies behind it; with its high, open timber roof and stained glass windows, it makes going to the pictures in Salisbury a unique experience. Watson's, the long-established glass and china business occupying the site in 1913, moved to Queen Street in 1931.

We were much delighted with Salisbury, especially the Close, with its fine elms, green meadows and old red-brick houses … Several have steps and curious old ironwork railings and gateways. I was much pleased with a sundial on the side of a house, 'Life's but a walking shadow'. BEATRIX POTTER

Left: SALISBURY, YE HALLE OF JOHN HALLE 1913 65310P

Opposite above: SALISBURY, HIGH STREET GATE 1894 34872

Opposite below: SALISBURY, THE CLOSE 1906 56371

RAMSBURY – *A timeless village scene*

RAMSBURY was unique for a village of this size in that it had its own building society, formed in 1846; an elm was used as its emblem. It ceased trading only recently. Even less has changed in this scene in the old part of what is a very old small town – it had its own bishop at the beginning of the 10th century. Later Frith photographs from the 1950s show almost no changes to these charming cottages. Note the small windows dictated by the timber framing, and the swooping thatched roofs.

Above: RAMSBURY, BURDETT STREET 1906 57200

BUCKLERS HARD – *A shipbuilding community*

THIS PICTURESQUE VILLAGE, part of the Beaulieu Estate, had its beginnings in the early 18th century, when the 2nd Duke of Montagu planned to build a free port, Montagu Town, here. He owned sugar plantations in the West Indies, and he wanted to import and export his sugar. By 1724 plans for a sizeable town had been drawn up, a road to the Beaulieu River constructed, and a few houses built. But his plans came to nothing, and Montagu Town remained a hamlet. In the early 19th century, the village (now known as Bucklers Hard) found a new role: about 50 wooden ships were built here for the Royal Navy, including three which fought at Trafalgar: the 'Agamemnon', the 'Eurylus', and the 'Swiftsure'. These cottages were the homes of the shipwrights, and the Master Shipbuilder, Henry Adams, lived in the handsome house at the end of the row. With the advent of iron ships, Bucklers Hard became a sleepy rural village again, popular with yachtsmen. Today, the fifth cottage down from the start of the terrace, No 84, is a chapel, and No 74 is the village shop. The Master Shipbuilder's house is now a hotel. Opposite these cottages is another almost identical row. Two and a half miles up the river is Beaulieu.

Left: BUCKLERS HARD, WEST TERRACE C1960   B43057

ANNA VALLEY
– *Hampshire brick and flint*

ANN or Anna was originally the name for the shining stream now known as the Pillhill Brook, a tributary of the River Anton. Here we see pleasing groups of cottages built in bands of brick and flint, with deep thatch and dormers – brick and flint is a characteristic building material in this area. It looks as if the house in the foreground is an early timber-framed building with a newer front. Roses are growing around the doors. To the north-west lies Weyhill, famous for its large country fair dating back to the 13th century.

Right: ANNA VALLEY,
LITTLE ANN VILLAGE C1955   A53006

ANDOVER – *Anton Mill, a pleasing Georgian brick building*

ANTON MILL stood on the River Anton, a tributary of the River Test, beside Barlows Lane. This pleasant Georgian brick building with a tiled roof was taken over by Hovis in 1914. Flour milling was then run down; by 1953, the mill was only producing animal feed. In the early 1960s the mill was demolished, and the site was redeveloped by Locomotors to produce security and other special vehicles.

Above: ANDOVER, ANTON MILL, 1906 54631P

RINGWOOD – *Cottage by the millstream*

ACCORDING to Domesday Book, Ringwood's mill was quite profitable, paying 22s in revenue. Before the Norman Conquest this land was held by Earl Tostig, but four hides of land from the original ten were seized for the creation of the Norman hunting forest. This fine view over the River Avon shows a horse cooling itself by the ancient ford and a thatcher practising his age-old craft on one of Ringwood's most picturesque cottages. The millstream was once much wider and prone to flooding. These thatched cottages were very susceptible to the floods, with the waters sometimes reaching up to the market place. One can imagine how the street outside must have been a sea of mud, with the townsfolk having to slop out their floors. By the 1950s (see below) the timbers on the front façade had been exposed, doubtless in the mistaken idea that this would bring authentic historical character.

[RINGWOOD] IS *situated on the border of the New Forest, on the eastern bank of the river Avon, which, after dividing eastward into three branches, over each of which is a stone bridge, again unites its waters into a broad expanse, with an island in the middle, crossed by a causeway. The town is well built and lighted with gas, and contains many neat residences ... A large portion of the land is in meadow, but the lower grounds frequently suffer from inundation, caused by the overflow of the Avon.*

'NATIONAL GAZETTEER OF GREAT BRITAIN AND IRELAND', 1868

Above: RINGWOOD, WEST STREET C1955   R35045
Left: RINGWOOD, THE MILLSTREAM 1900   45027P

SELBORNE – *The Wakes, home of the naturalist Gilbert White*

THE NATURALIST Gilbert White was born in Selborne in 1720. Though he lived in the village for most of his life, it was not until 1763 that The Wakes became his own house. White was passionate about the building, which adjoined the village street. In his time it was considerably smaller, and various wings and extensions have been added since the mid 19th century – the original parts are in light-coloured stone to the right. However, it is the garden that draws the whole harmoniously together, and a series of exquisite lawns and beds, created and lovingly tended by White and Thomas Hoar his gardener, extend out into the fields towards the Hanger, the high chalk hill that looms over Selborne to the south. It was in The Wakes that this gentle and modest country curate wrote the work that made him world-famous, 'The Natural History of Selborne'. It is the fourth most published book in the English language.

Mr White's own house, the successive abode of several generations of his family, is, of course, the first object of the traveller's inquiry. It stands not very far from the church, and is an irregular, unpretending edifice, which has evidently been enlarged at different periods, with more care of interior comfort than of architectural symmetry. Aided by the old-fashioned neatness of its lawns and gravel walks, the house preserves the staid aspect of bygone days, and has apparently undergone no alteration since the death of the naturalist. It was impossible to gaze on the spot without recalling to memory those hundred little passages in his book which, with so pleasing and beautiful an association, have identified the intellectual pursuits of the man, with the tasteful purity of his mind, with the every beauty of his beloved retreat.

'NEW MONTHLY MAGAZINE', C1850

Above: SELBORNE, THE WAKES 1898   42279

EVERSLEY – *The Rectory, home of Charles Kingsley*

THE WRITER Charles Kingsley wrote 'The Water Babies' while he lived in this old rectory. Kingsley and his wife are buried in the churchyard. Just behind lies Eversley church, over which Kingsley presided as rector.

Above: EVERSLEY, THE RECTORY, KINGSLEY'S STUDY 1901   46839

He and his wife now settled in the Rectory at Eversley; and life flowed on peacefully, notwithstanding the anxieties of a sorely neglected parish, and the expenses of an old house which had not been repaired for more than a hundred years. Owing to the circumstances under which the living fell vacant, the incoming tenant got no dilapidation-money, and had arrears of poor rates and the pay of his predecessor's curate to meet. The house was damp and unwholesome, surrounded with ponds, which overflowed with every heavy rain, and flooded not only the garden and stables, but all the rooms on the ground floor, keeping up master and servants sometimes all night baling out the water in buckets for hours together; and drainage works had to be done before it was habitable.

FROM 'CHARLES KINGSLEY: HIS LETTERS AND MEMORIES',
EDITED BY HIS WIFE, 1879

ODIHAM – *Tudor timber and Georgian brick*

ODIHAM'S houses are a mixture of Georgian and Tudor; some are timber-framed, which was common before local bricks came into general use in the 18th century. The Priory and neighbouring Palace Gate Farm were once part of a Tudor palace visited by Queen Elizabeth I.

The 18th- and early 19th-century cottages on the left face the timber-framed house, which was built as a single dwelling in 1540; it is continuously jettied with a hearth-passage entrance - in other words, an internal chimney stack is positioned behind the entrance. By 1834, when it was known as Kings Barn Farm, it had been divided into three dwellings. Note the coal hole, bottom right.

Right: ODIHAM, OLD HOUSES,
CEMETERY HILL 1910   63011

ALBURY – *Augustus Pugin's spectacular chimneys adorning old cottages*

ALBURY is situated in the gentle rolling scenery of the Tillingbourne valley. The first thing we notice in this photograph is the chimneys, which seem out of proportion to the cottages. Albury is famous for its chimneys: the great house, Albury Park, originally timber-framed, was virtually rebuilt in the 17th century, and has 63 chimneys. Ornate chimneys also dominate several of the buildings in the village, including the ones in this photograph. They were designed by Augustus Pugin while he was making alterations to Albury Park following its acquisition in 1819 by Henry Drummond, a wealthy banker and MP; thanks to Pugin's alterations, the cottages have taken on a neo-Gothic, picturesque look. They are all now private houses, but one of them was once a haberdasher's, then a doctor's surgery, and later a chemist's. One of the windows, dating from the 18th century, came from Steventon Manor (Steventon was Jane Austen's birthplace). Another of the houses is called Farrier's Cottage – the building opposite used to be the forge.

Above: ALBURY, THE VILLAGE C1950 A25070P

DORKING – *A tile-hung backwater*

AN ENCHANTING CORNER of old Dorking: the photographer has captured a moment with two people standing in their respective doorways, and a cat sitting on the left looking at the bearded man. Note the cobble stones, the pot plants, the juxtaposition of roof-lines – and the Victorian hung tiles on the right. Note, too, the huge gas lamp and the trade sign on the right; both advertise the business of J Chart, an undertaker. The hale and hearty old man looks far from needing his services.

Left: DORKING, CAPE PLACE 1913   65212

EAST HORSLEY – *Horsley Towers*

THIS WONDERFULLY eccentric mock Rhenish Gothic castle was created by Lord Lovelace, who bought the original house on this site in 1840 and spent thirty years transforming the building; the house was renamed Horsley Towers after he added the amazing tower in 1858. Lovelace was an enthusiastic builder and inventor. He pioneered the technique of bending wood by steaming, and his great hall was built in 1847 using beams shaped in this way – no less a personage than Isambard Kingdom Brunel was impressed. Lovelace was also enthusiastic about making bricks, and he won the medal for brick making at the Great Exhibition of 1851. He left his mark on the village and elsewhere by building a medley of fine brick and flint cottages, and he also built a number of characteristic horseshoe-shaped bridges. From 1919 to 1926, Horsley Towers belonged to Sir Thomas Sopwith, the aircraft designer and yachtsman.

Right: EAST HORSLEY, HORSLEY TOWERS C1955   H120013

BLETCHINGLEY – *Place Farm, once a Tudor gatehouse*

BEFORE 1582, documents referred to this village as 'Blechingley', meaning 'the ley (or clearing) of the Blaecci people', and its origins probably date back to the 7th or 8th century. Even today, some residents are opposed to the introduction of the 't' into its name. The house at Place Farm was once the gatehouse of Bletchingley Place; this was a great Tudor house, and Anne of Cleves lived here after her divorce from Henry VIII. Behind the 18th-century porch we can see the remains of a very large and grand Tudor entrance, and elsewhere on the façade we can see evidence of blocked and altered windows – altogether a rather unsubtle conversion!

Above left: BLETCHINGLEY, PLACE FARM 1907   57498

Below left: CLOSE UP OF THE TUDOR ENTRANCE 1907

Below right: BLETCHINGLEY, THE WHYTE HART, A CHIMNEY CORNER 1907 57494

HERE WE SEE how the heart of the English house used to be. The great fireplace takes up most of one side of the room. From the mighty beam hangs a patterned valence, which would help increase the up-draught. To each side of the inglenook are cosy seats, and around the fire are ranged bellows, tongs, poker, scuttle and a warming pan. In pride of place is a cast iron fire back dated 1613, flanked by a pair of fire dogs.

CAMBERLEY AND FRIMLEY – *Rampant creeper, the evidence of neglect*

THESE PICTURES show how vulnerable and fragile old cottages can be. All too often, once the roof has deteriorated, the rest of the house follows. In the photograph of Frimley, a creeper has invaded the thatch; however, the thatch itself looks in reasonable condition, and the chimney looks relatively new. The donkey and the children look happy and well fed – poverty does not appear to have struck this family, and decay has not gone too far yet. However, in the photograph of the cottage in Camberley, it looks as if the roof has completely collapsed under the weight of creeper. Yet there are curtains in the window on the left, and the shrubs in the garden are neatly clipped.

Above: FRIMLEY GREEN, AN OLD COTTAGE 1906 54907P

Left: CAMBERLEY, OLD COTTAGE 1906 57181

LEWES – *Ann of Cleves's house*

THIS BEAUTIFUL tile-hung Wealden hall house was given to Anne of Cleves by Henry VIII as part of their divorce settlement; however, Anne of Cleves never lived here. It is now a museum, and its fascinating collections include farming and domestic artefacts assembled by private individuals, including the collection of the Lewes ironfounder J E Every. These artefacts formed the basis of the important reference work 'Iron and Brass Implements of the English House' by J Seymour Lindsay, published in 1916. The museum also covers the Wealden iron industry, Tudor gunfounding, and the story of Lewes from the 16th century to the present day. Note the bands of round and diamond-shaped tiles on the façade, and the chequered stone and flint of the porch.

At the end of the valley rose the town of Lewes on its hill, blue and mysterious in the misty, shimmering heat ... There are elegant 18th-century-looking houses, and ancient intricate houses built of flints. The castle is of flint, and from its towers you can look down on the roofs of Lewes ... On the way out of Lewes I looked about for a pitch, but it was not until I reached the bottom of the town, among the rows of cottages, a little world of flint cottages, half-timbered cottages, and decoratively tiled cottages, that I put up the [Punch and Judy] show in a grubby side-street.

WALTER WILKINSON, 'A SUSSEX PEEP-SHOW',
GEOFFREY BLES 1933

Right: LEWES, SOUTHOVER, ANNE OF CLEVES'S HOUSE 1898   41917

ALFRISTON – *The Clergy House, the first National Trust property*

Above: A TYPICAL TIMBER-FRAME CONSTRUCTION

Above: ALFRISTON, THE CLERGY HOUSE 1894   34494   *Below:* ALFRISTON, THE CLERGY HOUSE 1921   71427

THE CLERGY HOUSE was built in about 1350. It was the first property acquired by the National Trust, who paid £10 for it in 1896 - and then spent another £300 to restore it. It is a rare survival of a 14th-century thatched Wealden hall house. Possibly originally a farmhouse, the low, timber-framed building later became known as the Clergy House when it passed into the possession of the church as a home for local priests. The lofty central hall is the hub of the building; it rises up to the rafters. On either side of it are two-storey blocks, one of which contained the retiring room and solar. The roof beams bear a carving of oak leaves – were they the origin of the National Trust symbol? The floor is made of rammed chalk, a traditional surface made of chalk pounded to make a smooth surface, and sealed with soured milk. The photographs show the house during and after restoration.

WINCHELSEA, despite its status, is the smallest town in England; it is really little more than a village, and it feels like a prosperous garden suburb with its grass verges and widely-spaced houses. Winchelsea is an 'ancient town', like Rye, equal in status to the Cinque Ports, and had a duty to provide a quota of ships for the English fleet.

Winchelsea was laid out as a 'new town' in 1288 on the hilltop when the original town was claimed by the sea in 1287. The town was planned in a gridiron pattern with 39 blocks, but today it covers only 12 of the original blocks. The Armoury has a chequered history. It was built in 1764 by the English Linen Company as a 'manufactory' of cambric and lawns. The building accommodated 160 spinners, winders and weavers and 26 apprentices, superintended by a Frenchman, Monsieur Mariteau; there were 86 looms. Later it became the Bear Inn. It acquired its present name during the Napoleonic Wars, when troops of the Duke of Wellington's army were quartered nearby. Later in the 19th century Miss Maud Peel, niece of Sir Robert Peel, rebuilt the house to convert it to a private dwelling.

Below: WINCHELSEA, THE ARMOURY 1906 53491

WINCHELSEA – *The Armoury, once an 18th-century textile manufactory*

RYE – *Ancient port, and harmonious medley of architectural styles*

'LIKE OTHER maritime towns, [Rye] smells of fish and punch'. So said John Byng, who made several excursions round Britain in the 1780s and 90s. The old hospital on the right in the photograph opposite (21161), so called since it performed that function during the Napoleonic Wars, forms the main subject of this early picture of the most photographed of Rye's cobbled streets, which slopes downhill towards Strand Quay. Its historic buildings, ranging from medieval half-timbering to Georgian brick, are well preserved today.

This delightful street is named after the watch bell which hung here and was rung to warn inhabitants of approaching French raids. The street was haunted until the Second World War by the hurrying footsteps of an uneasy little ghost. The steps were never heard again after an Elizabethan house was bombed out and a workman found a string of beads. They were in fact rare black pearls, lost here by one of Elizabeth I's ladies in 1573. Swan House in Watchbell Street became Mallards, Georgie Pillson's home, for the television production of E F Benson's 'Lucia' novels about Tilling-on-Sea. Trellis was carefully added to hide a garage. Note the pleasing variety of building styles and materials in this street: timber framing, tile hanging, and plain brick cottages, some embellished with later bay windows, and roofs of all pitches and shapes.

Rye, upon its promontory above estuaries yet navigable – though its marine commerce has migrated in great part to a newer settlement upon the shore – is thickly crowded together, roof rising above roof, around the old church, whose low tower crowns the hill. With streets narrow and tortuous, paved in many places with pebbles from the beach, it has all the aspect of a medieval fortified town.   VICTORIAN GUIDEBOOK, C1890

Opposite left: RYE, MERMAID STREET 1888 21161

Above right: RYE, WATCHBELL STREET 1912 64932

BODIAM is a 14th-century moated castle, restored, like Tattershall in Lincolnshire, by Lord Curzon in 1919. It had been a ruin since a brief siege in the Civil War in 1643. The original approach was along a wooden bridge at right angles to the castle walls, thus exposing an attacker's unshielded flank to fire from the defenders. Details are difficult to make out in this pre-restoration photograph but in front of the gateway tower is the ruined barbican, and in front of that is the much overgrown octagonal island, which at one time might also have been fortified. Bodiam was protected by three drawbridges, two fortified bastions, three portcullises, and an internal arrangement of rooms and doorways designed for defence. It has been impeccably restored, and is now in the stewardship of the National Trust. In this atmospheric photograph, the romantic pile of grey stone, draped with ivy, appears to float serenely above its moat.

Right: BODIAM, THE CASTLE 1890 25390

BODIAM – *Bodiam Castle, 14th-century moated stronghold*

CRANBROOK – *A Wealden hall house*

SOME KENTISH villages expanded in medieval times by having a thriving local industry. A good example is Cranbrook. Flemish weavers came here in the 14th century, and made the village a centre of medieval cloth making, using wool from the local flocks. The long main street, the Hill, is bordered by tile-hung or weather-boarded cottages. Situated on the High Street is the Studio, a Wealden hall house, with a later gable on the left-hand side, probably originally built for a prosperous weaver. This photograph was taken before restoration; note that the building is divided into several houses. The building, now called the Old Studio, is unchanged today, but has been thoroughly restored. It gained its name from the Victorian artist Thomas Webster, a member of the Cranbrook colony of artists, who lived and painted in the house. He is remembered for being hauled round the town in a bath-chair by a donkey with an artificial tail.

Left: CRANBROOK, THE STUDIO 1901 46432

ICKHAM – *An ancient brick rectory with Flemish details*

THE 17TH-CENTURY scholar Meric Casaubon lived in this rectory. This fine building shows a pleasing mix of different styles. On the left we can see medieval stonework and windows, whilst a Flemish influence seems apparent on the right of the building – note the crow-stepped gables. The earliest parts date from the 13th century. The house is now a nursing home set in three acres of gardens. Ickham itself is one of the villages of the Little Stour; it consists of a pleasant mixture of weatherboard, brick and tile-hung dwellings. There was once a mill on the stream here. Mains water did not arrive until 1913, with gas following in 1926 and electricity in 1931.

KENNINGTON – *Timber, brick and tile combined*

THIS is a 16th-century building par excellence, much altered and added to down the centuries. It is timber-framed, tile-hung and jettied, and bears a cluster of tall chimneys. The brickwork is English bond, often used to build thicker and stronger walls. In 1895 there were brick and tile works in the village, continuing the long tradition of building using local materials. Sad to say, Kennington is not very rural now; it has become ever more just a suburb of Ashford. The church has a fantastically old yew tree next to the churchyard, reliably dated to be around 2,000 years old.

DURING the 16th and 17th centuries, Huguenot weavers from France and Walloon weavers from the Low Countries emigrated to England to escape religious persecution. Many of them settled in Canterbury, where they were given the right to trade by Elizabeth I. It is said that about a hundred families came to Canterbury at this time; with them they brought their looms and their skill, which was one of the main reasons that Canterbury became a centre for the weaving trade. The woven fabrics made here were of silk, cotton and wool. Those weavers are not forgotten in Canterbury today thanks to the houses where they used to work; these picturesque back street cottages, just off the High Street, hang over the River Stour. Today they are still in use as shops, restaurants and the Weavers public house.

CANTERBURY – *Weavers' cottages on the Stour*

Above left: ICKHAM, THE OLD RECTORY C1960 11021

Below left: KENNINGTON, AN OLD COTTAGE 1901 47542

Above: CANTERBURY, WEAVERS' COTTAGES FROM KING'S BRIDGE 1921 70331A

SMALLHYTHE – *The actress Ellen Terry's home*

THIS is a fascinating little village with some interesting buildings. Smallhythe was a harbour as late as the 16th century, when the sea came up this far from Rye. Here we can see the small church, rebuilt in brick to a Flemish design after the original church was burned down in 1514; beyond it stands the attractive black and white timber-framed Priests House. Further down the lane we can see another house, Smallhythe Place, also timber-framed, and with a steeply pitched red-tiled roof – it was built in 1480. This was once the home of the harbour master, which shows just how far the sea used to come up during the Middle Ages. The actress Ellen Terry lived in the house from 1919 until her death in 1928. The house is now in the care of the National Trust, and open to the public. It contains a collection of memorabilia, including Garrick's stool, a girdle once owned by Sarah Bernhardt, and a variety of playbills from Ellen Terry's performances in theatres all over Britain.

Above: SMALLHYTHE, ELLEN TERRY'S HOUSE C1955 S701070

Left: SMALLHYTHE, THE VILLAGE 1900 45007

LONDON – *Cheyne Walk, handsome Georgian brick terraces, the homes of celebrated artists and writers*

A CARRIAGE with a top-hatted coachman waits patiently outside one of Cheyne Walk's many grand Georgian brick houses. This elegant street of handsome dwellings was built in 1708. Graceful plane trees screen residents from the more boisterous life on the water. A fleet of barges, their sales furled, squat in the mud alongside the quay. Before the Chelsea Embankment was constructed in 1874, Cheyne Walk was a pleasant riverside promenade; now the London traffic thunders by. The street was a centre of Chelsea literary and artistic talent in the 19th century. George Eliot lived for a short while at the very end of her life at No 4. Dante Gabriel Rossetti, the poet and painter (a founder member of the Pre-Raphaelite Brotherhood), and the poets Algernon Swinburne and George Meredith moved into No 16 (Queen's House) in 1862. Henry James lived at Carlyle Mansions, Mrs Gaskell at No 93, the painter James McNeill Whistler at No 96, and Hilaire Belloc at No 104. The painter J M W Turner lived incognito at No 119. Carlyle lived here too, and William Allingham recalls visiting him in 1867 (see below right):

Above: LONDON, CHEYNE WALK 1890   L130087

WEDNESDAY 16TH OCTOBER: *Cheyne Walk – call at Carlyle's. When the door opens, see him in the passage; he says in an angry voice – 'Go away, sir! I can do nothing with you.' I go away, with reflections many and black. What can it mean?*

THURSDAY 17TH OCTOBER: *Very kind letter from Carlyle – did not know me that day I called; 'must blame my poor old eyes. Allingham's company would have been very welcome to me.' How I have tormented myself!*

WILLIAM ALLINGHAM, 'DIARIES', 1867

Left: LONDON, CHEYNE WALK 1890   L130084

LONDON – *Park Lane, fashionable street of aristocratic great houses*

UNTIL the end of the 18th century, London was a compact city. Its merchants lived in the square mile, and the aristocracy in the more fashionable areas of Piccadilly and the West End. Beyond Park Lane, however, there was a wilderness of forest and mire, where footpads and highwaymen lurked. Londoners were regularly accosted in the Strand. Many preferred to travel by water on the River Thames. Park Lane, once the desolate by-road known as Tiburn Lane, was a refined street of palatial mansions enjoying expansive vistas of Hyde Park. These great houses included Grosvenor House, the home of the Marquess of Westminster, Holdernesse House, the residence of the Marquess of Londonderry, and Dorchester House.

LONDON – *An early mobile home*

VAGRANTS have wandered the fields and lanes of Britain down the centuries. Subject to no laws, they were the truly free people of the world. The Vagrancy Act of 1824 made it illegal for them to be out in the open air without visible means of subsistence. Life became suddenly more regulated and less free. Families followed the country fairs and markets, and often ventured into London for the festivals and fairs held on the commons. The caravan in the photograph could very well be an early Reading-style wagon, with its ribbed construction clearly visible and a plain arched roof (later Reading wagons had a skylight in the roof). This style of wagon was pioneered by the Dunton family in Reading in Berkshire, but was copied by other builders. Travellers and gypsies were often itinerant traders and craftsmen, offering brushes, baskets, mats and metalware.

Above:
LONDON,
PARK LANE
1890
L130166P

Right:
LONDON,
NOMADS 1885
L130212P

WOKINGHAM – *Timber-framed houses remodelled*

WOKINGHAM was for centuries within the bounds of Windsor Forest. Strict forest laws were applied, and this influenced the way in which the area developed. The forest was a hunting ground and a valuable source of timber, which, as we can clearly see here, was much needed for building. Wokingham became established with the granting of a market charter in 1219. Today a significant number of buildings survive from the 15th century, and their quality suggests a relatively prosperous way of life for some. During the 18th century, although new houses were built, many of the existing timber-framed houses were modernised by the addition of a brick façade with sash windows and panelled doors. In the days when the photograph was taken, the young girl with her large wooden hoop could use the street as a playground with little fear from traffic. The timber-framed buildings behind her were eventually demolished. Today the site is occupied by new housing, and Cross Street (emerging near the gas lamp in this photograph) has been re-routed.

Left: WOKINGHAM, ROSE STREET 1906 57028

Below: BRAY, JESUS HOSPITAL 1890 23624

A FORMER royal manor, Bray is well known for the song 'The Vicar of Bray', celebrating the vicar who changed sides several times during the Civil War to keep his living.

The tranquillity of this delightful village is disturbed by heavy traffic, like many in the area. Jesus Hospital is a fine quadrangle of 28 single-storey almshouses with a taller entrance bay. It was founded in 1627 by William Goddard, a local man made good – he was a citizen of London and a member of the Fishmongers Company. He is commemorated with a statue, and his monument is in the church.

Thirty-four of the disadvantaged poor of Bray and six of the Fishmongers Company were housed here. A stern notice in the entrance archway states that 'Vagrants, Hawkers and Dogs Are Not Admitted'. The building still stands proudly in the village with William Goddard's effigy above the entrance.

BRAY – *Jesus Hospital, 17th-century almshouses*

CLIVEDEN – *Cliveden House, opulent Victorian mansion*

BETWEEN COOKHAM and Boulters Lock, the River Thames cuts close to the Buckinghamshire bank to form beautiful tree-clad river cliffs rising 150 feet to the chalk plateau above. This is widely regarded as one of the most beautiful stretches of the Thames. Cliveden benefits from a breathtaking river view from its terraces. The first house was built in the 1660s by the 2nd Duke of Buckingham as a hunting lodge and for entertaining his friends. Since then it has twice burnt down; today's Cliveden is an opulent Victorian mansion designed for the Duke of Sutherland by Sir Charles Barry, one of the architects of the Houses of Parliament, and completed in 1851. Owned by the Astor family since the 1890s, Cliveden became famous as the hub for the socialite 'Cliveden Set', and in the 1960s for the Profumo and Christine Keeler scandal. The magnificent house is now a country house hotel, and is maintained by the National Trust.

The 'castled crags' of the Rhine and the Moselle, – the 'blue rushing of the arrowy Rhone,' – the massive grandeur of the banks of the Danube, are far more imposing and stimulating; but the quiet, tranquil loveliness of this part of the Thames may make good its claim to take rank even with those world-famed rivers. There is something both unique and charming in the dry 'combes,' or fissures in the chalk ranges, rapidly descending and garnished with sweeping foliage of untrimmed beech trees. The branches gracefully bend down to the slope of the rising sward; while, from the steepness of the angle, the tree-tops appear from below as a succession of pinnacles against the sky. Many a roamer through distant lands has come home to give the palm for the perfection of natural beauty to the rocks and hanging woods of Cliefden. That they are within an hour's run of London does not indeed abate their claim to admiration, but may suggest the reason why they are so comparatively little known.

THE REV SAMUEL MANNING, 1885

Above: CLIVEDEN HOUSE 1893   31758

SONNING – *Flower-bedecked lock-side cottages on the River Thames*

PRONOUNCED 'SUNNING', the village of Sonning is full of charm and character. Many Georgian and timber-framed cottages line its streets. Edward Hudson, the owner of 'Country Life', lived in the village in a house designed for him by Sir Edwin Lutyens in 1901. The Thames falls gently by 4 feet at Sonning Lock. A short distance from here, the river is crossed by a bridge which is understood to be the oldest on the Thames. Colourful flowerbeds and borders line the banks, and, on a fine day, the towpath is invariably packed with visitors.

Is there a spot more lovely than the rest,
By art improved, by nature truly blest?
A noble river at its base running,
It is a little village known as Sonning.

JAMES SADLER, POET, AND SONNING LOCK KEEPER (1845-1885)

Above: SONNING, THE LOCK 1917   67959

Above: ABINGDON, EAST ST HELEN STREET 1890   26996

ABINGDON – *Chequered brick and royal connections*

ABINGDON is a fine historic town given added quality by its river frontage. It has a superb collection of historic buildings, ranging from the medieval abbey gateway, the parish church of St Helen, and Briock Alley Almshouses, to the Town Hall of 1677. Many fine Tudor, Stuart and Georgian houses line its attractive streets. Note the house halfway down the street on the left with six windows and a central pedimented doorcase. This is Unicorn House, No 28, which had its moment in history. In December 1688 William of Orange, the Dutch ruler, stayed the night here on his way to London from Torbay, having been offered the crown in place of the Catholic James II. He was the guest of the house's owner, Thomas Medlycott. On the right of the photo we see how a Georgian builder has created a dramatic effect using vitrified headers (bricks fired to the point of blue glassiness and set head-on) in a chequered pattern.

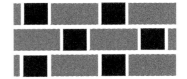

BANBURY – *Broughton Castle, Tudor home of the Lords Saye and Sele*

Above: BROUGHTON CASTLE 1922   72110

BROUGHTON CASTLE was built as a fortified manor house by Sir John de Broughton in the 14th century. Sir Thomas Wykeham converted the house into a castle in 1406 – at this time battlements were added to the gatehouse. In the 15th century Broughton passed by marriage to the Fiennes family, and in 1554 Richard Fiennes considerably enlarged the house. After his death his son Richard continued the decoration of the interior, recording the date 1599 on the magnificent plaster ceiling in the Great Parlour. Thus during the Elizabethan era the house was transformed into the Tudor mansion we see today. In the 17th century Broughton became a gathering point for the Parliamentarians; William, 8th Lord Saye and Sele raised forces which fought at the nearby Battle of Edgehill in 1642. In the early 19th century, William Thomas, 15th Lord Saye and Sele, indulged in a life of frivolity and extravagance. The family then lived in Erith in Kent, and neglected the castle; in 1837 the contents of the castle were sold, even including the swans on the moat. However, the loss of the family fortune in the Regency period almost certainly saved Broughton from Victorian 'restoration'. William Thomas's successor, Frederick, carried out vital repair work in the 1860s under the direction of the architect George Gilbert Scott, and in the 20th century further extensive restoration has taken place.

The bedrooms are clean and convenient, with good old chimney-pieces and nice oaken floors: the chimney-piece in the king's bedchamber, where King Charles lay in several of his marches, is of the superb style. But the ornaments of the house are the dining-and drawing-rooms, which are noble apartments of complete proportion with lofty chimney-pieces. The entrance into the dining-room I much admired, and the ceiling of the drawing-room is one of the most beautiful I ever saw, a model for such work.

JOHN BYNG, 1785 ('RIDES ROUND BRITAIN', EDITED D ADAMSON, FOLIO SOCIETY)

MAPLEDURHAM – *Ancient Thameside watermill*

WATERMILLS were usually constructed of local building materials, and reflect the agricultural prosperity of a locality. The wheels were always in motion, which caused considerable wear and tear, and reconstruction usually occurred every fifty years or so; thus watermill buildings were continuously altered over the years. Both the mill building and its machinery were inextricably linked to the milling process. A mill is part home and part machine, and the two functions are inseparable. This 15th-century brick and timber building with a tiled roof on the River Thames has a prominent sack hoist lantern projecting above the roofline. As we can see, two low breastshot waterwheels power the mill. A turbine later replaced the left-hand waterwheel. A horse-drawn water cart, in the foreground, is being filled from the river, while the horse cools its feet in the shallows; it is interesting to consider for what purpose the river water was being collected. The mill, which is open to visitors, is now restored to working order using one waterwheel, and regularly produces flour. It is now the only working corn and grist watermill left on the Thames.

Above: MAPLEDURHAM, THE MILL AND THE CHURCH 1892   27092
Right: MAPLEDURHAM, THE MILL 1890   27091P

CROPREDY – *A floating home on the Oxford Canal*

THE OXFORD CANAL is a pretty, meandering waterway, very popular with holidaymakers. This view shows an early example of a houseboat on the Oxford Canal. It has been moored here for a while, because a plant is growing up the windows. Saunders, the name of the company which used to own it, is painted on the bow. As inexpensive homes, converted narrowboats are still popular, especially closer to Oxford, where there are dozens to be seen.

Left: CROPREDY,
THE OXFORD CANAL C1960   C291006P

Below right: GRENDON UNDERWOOD,
CRUCKS C1960   G230005

GRENDON UNDERWOOD is a long, straggling Buckinghamshire village, with the gaps filled steadily from the 1950s onwards. The name of this cottage is a reminder of a very important medieval and late medieval building tradition in this area, possibly associated with the abundance of oak trees in the Bernwood Forest and its surroundings. A cruck is best described as a curving A-frame, a pair of massive timbers that run from the ground to the apex of the roof, usually cut from the same tree. Long Crendon has over 20 cruck houses, an unusual concentration, but many of the villages round about have a few – Haddenham has four and Grendon Underwood two, for example. Often hidden behind render, as here, they are still being discovered.

Right:
PLAN OF CRUCK
CONSTRUCTION

GRENDON UNDERWOOD – *Hidden cruck construction*

HIGH WYCOMBE – *Pleasing spacious villas for the Victorian commuter*

SITUATED in the narrow valley of the River Wye, this medieval borough developed into a major corn market. The arrival of the furniture industry, based on the 18th-century planting of the Chiltern beech woods, led to considerable Victorian expansion from the original Georgian core. Amersham Hill was part of the Victorian expansion. Laid out in the late 19th century, it replaced a turnpike that climbed the hill further west. Near the railway station, it sprouted Victorian houses and villas for commuters and Wycombe citizens alike. These pleasing semi-detached houses would have been lived in by commuters to London and by the town's middle classes. Their rooms must have seemed spacious with their high ceilings and bays with large windows, which allowed the light to flood in and brighten the interiors embellished with mouldings and cornices. Built of industrially-manufactured Victorian bricks, houses like this were a template for the future. Similar ones could be seen in suburbs all over London – no longer was there a prevailing local vernacular. Builders now worked with fewer and fewer traditional pattern books.

Above: HIGH WYCOMBE, AMERSHAM HILL 1906   53668

WADDESDON – *Waddesdon Manor, Baron Rothschild's French chateau fantasy*

NOW OWNED by the National Trust, Waddesdon Manor is a massive French chateau deposited on a windswept hilltop for Baron Ferdinand de Rothschild. Rothschild used a French architect, the splendidly-named Hippolyte Alexandre Gabriel Walter Destailleur. The work took from 1877 to 1899, and was finished by Destailleur's son, André. The photograph above shows the wonderfully ornate and utterly French garden front. When Ferdinand Rothschild bought the estate, the hill was virtually devoid of trees; he imported vast numbers of mature trees to create its present wooded character, teams of horses toiling to haul their huge loads up the hill. Rothschild had the grounds landscaped with parterres close to the house, rock mounds, statuary, fountains and the superb aviary (left), a copy of one from near his childhood home in Germany. It dates from 1889, and combines the aviary with a grotto crammed with Italian statuary.

Above: WADDESDON, WADDESDON MANOR, THE SOUTH FRONT 1897 39653

Left: WADDESDON, WADDESDON MANOR, THE AVIARY 1897 39663

BUCKINGHAM – *Quirky barley-twist chimneys*

Above: BUCKINGHAM, THE MANOR HOUSE, A TWISTED CHIMNEY C1955
B280035

MAIDS MORETON – *Contrasting cottage styles*

THE 'MAIDS' in the village name were the unmarried Peover sisters, who endowed and rebuilt the superb Perpendicular parish church around 1450. Maids Moreton is a curious village, with large numbers of small 17th- and 18th-century cottages, many constructed of rather flimsy timber-framing, contrasting with a very few grand Victorian houses. Here we see another contrast in architectural styles. North of Main Street, the dignified 1950s council housing was built on The Leys field. As with so many council house developments, they were built on land at the fringes of the village, and inhabitants enjoyed superb views over the surrounding countryside. In the foreground Old Page's Cottage is another of Maids Moreton's late timber-framed cottages, with thin timbers and a thatched roof.

Above: MAIDS MORETON, THE LEYS C1955   M264012

A DISASTROUS FIRE in 1725 destroyed about a third of the town, and many buildings date from after the fire. The Market Square (actually rectangular) achieved Georgian grandeur by the end of the century. Frith's photographer has caught a delightful quirky chimney on the north side of the Manor House in Church Street, a chimney much drawn and photographed by others. The Manor House was originally built as a house for a Lincoln Cathedral prebendary - Buckingham was then in Lincoln diocese. Mostly 16th-century, the north wing is graced by this spiral brick chimney, supported for years by iron stays.

HARPENDEN – *Once a rural idyll, now absorbed by modern development*

SAD to relate, this restful scene of Cock Pond in Harpenden with its magnificent trees, thatched cottages and elegant pair of swans fell victim to the sweeping expansionism and development of the 20th century. The pond was drained and grassed over during the twenties as the 'highway valley' village grew into a 'garden town'. Such informal and unstructured villagescapes evolved slowly down the centuries, creating their own unique harmony; it is only lately that tarmac and housing developments have compromised their charm.

Above: HARPENDEN, THE VILLAGE POND 1897 39732

PANSHANGER was built in 1806 by Peter, 5th Earl Cowper on high ground close to the valley of the River Mimram. He was advised by Repton; the house was built on the site of an existing Elizabethan farmhouse in castellated Gothic style, using bricks made on site. Engravings of the 19th century show an elegant country mansion, fronted by broad swathes of lawn running down to a lake with sailing boats; Panshanger was a centre of culture and lavish entertaining. In 1855 the mansion narrowly escaped destruction by a fire which caused £12,000 worth of damage; however, the unique art collection that included works by Rembrandt, Van Dyck, Poussin, and Rubens was saved. In 1919, a large part of the estate was sold to Ebenezer Howard to become the site of Welwyn Garden City. Eventually, Panshanger passed to Lord Desborough, and when Lady Desborough died in 1955, the mansion was demolished. Only the stables now remain, and Repton's exquisite landscaping.

Right: HERTFORD, PANSHANGER HOUSE 1933 85564

HERTFORD – *Panshanger House*

RICKMANSWORTH – *Moor Park*

MOOR PARK was built in the 1720s for the banker and South Sea Bubble profiteer Benjamin Styles. It was designed by Sir James Thornhill, who had to sue Styles to get his fees paid. Thornhill was probably assisted by Giacomo Leoni, to whom the house is often attributed. It apparently cost Styles £130,000, several millions in modern money. The grand, imposing house is built in Portland stone, and has a gigantic Corinthian portico; situated on a hill, it overlooks a large landscaped park, reworked by Capability Brown in the 1750s. By the time this picture was taken, the arrival of the Metropolitan railway in the town ten years earlier had seen part of the extensive grounds sold for housing development. The house was no longer lived in after 1921, and more of the park was sold for housing in the 1930s. Today Moor Park serves as a clubhouse for the adjoining golf course and tennis courts.

Left: RICKMANSWORTH, MOOR PARK 1897 39686

THIS IMPOSING 17th-century mansion was originally designed by Sir Christopher Wren for Henry Guy, and was formerly a home of the Gore family, before being purchased by Lionel Rothschild, the MP and banker, for his son Nathaniel ('Natty') in 1872. The upper storey was added in 1890, and the old walls were encased with red brick and pediments in 1915. The morning room was panelled in exotic woods, with an elaborate fireplace and four built-in cupboards which housed Natty's impressive collection of objets d'art. His architect at Tring was William Huckvale, whose work can be seen throughout the village. Constance Battersea, a Rothschild cousin, said of Natty: 'Cottage building was one of his hobbies, and very comfortable and well-constructed his cottages are, with a low rental to recommend them ... He built four hundred at the very least on his estate.' Natty was a hospitable man, and there were many house parties at Tring Park; the guests included Randolph Churchill, the young Winston Churchill, the Gladstones, Cecil Rhodes and Edward VII, both as Prince of Wales and King. Natty's son, Lionel Walter, was an enthusiastic, if eccentric, collector of birds and animals; he kept many exotic animals in the park, including zebras and cassowaries.

TRING – *Tring Park*

Right: TRING, TRING PARK 1897 39651

HITCHIN – *The Biggin,*
priory, school and medieval almshouse

THE BIGGIN has housed many different kinds of people. It was originally built in 1361 by Sir Edward de Kendale as a Gilbertine priory. The present building is mostly 16th century, but parts of the older building survive – the window on the south front dates from the 14th century, for instance. The priory was dissolved in 1538, and the building became a private house; in one of the rooms, the panelling is carved with the date 1585 together with initials that may be those of William Croocar and his wife. From 1635 The Biggin was owned by Joseph Kempe, who used it as a school. In 1654 Kempe died, and left The Biggin on trust for the benefit of 'ten auncient or middle aged women' and 'four poor children of Hitchin to be apprentices in some honest occupation'. Although over the years it was also used as a poor house, The Biggin continued to house 'Kempe's widows'; by 1857, they had increased to eighteen, and the Hitchin Charity Trustees resolved that they should be each paid a shilling a week. In 1960, Kempe's Trustees handed The Biggin over to Hitchin Charities, who repaired and renovated the building. There are now twelve residents, who each have a bed-sitting room with a bathroom and kitchen. In the photograph, we see three of 'Kempe's widows' in the inner courtyard of The Biggin as it was at the turn of the century.

In the photograph opposite, the wall to the right seems to be constructed using English bond (see illustration below).

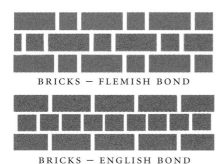

BRICKS – FLEMISH BOND

BRICKS – ENGLISH BOND

Left: HITCHIN, THE BIGGIN 1903 49742

Right: HITCHIN, THE BIGGIN 1903 49743P

TOTTERNHOE – *Timber-framing with brick infill*

THIS PRETTY SCENE with its unmetalled road and air of tranquillity could almost prevail in modern Totternhoe. Certainly many of the current properties in the village are thatched and show the timber-framed construction with brick infill used on the house in the foreground. Note the small windows on the first floor, their size dictated by the space between the timbers. Totternhoe Knolls is the name given to the remains of Totternhoe Castle, a motte and bailey over Saxon remains, of which only the foundations remain. The area is designated a Site of Special Scientific Interest and a Scheduled Ancient Monument.

Above: TOTTERNHOE, THE VILLAGE 1897 39754P

ELSTOW – *Home of the writer and preacher John Bunyan*

WHEN JOHN BUNYAN, the son of a brasier in the village, walked the lanes and fields of Elstow in the 17th century, it was an isolated village a mile and a half south of the King's Ditch around that part of Bedford south of the River Ouse. Now Bedford's housing estates, business parks and industrial estates have swallowed the fields and have reached the north end of the village; they have spread east and west, but so far have not engulfed Elstow. The majority of the buildings in the village are in whole or in part 17th-century in origin. Bunyan's birthplace, anachronistically covered in pebbledash at the time of this photograph, was demolished in 1968.

Left: ELSTOW, BUNYAN'S COTTAGE AND THE VILLAGE 1921   70453

There is the cottage which tradition identifies with Bunyan: with the church and the belfry, so memorable in the record of his experiences; the village green on which in his thoughtless youth he used to play at 'tip-cat:' there is nothing more to see; but it is impossible to pace through those homely ways without remembering how once the place was luminous to his awe-stricken spirit with 'the light that never was on sea or shore', and the landscape on which his inward eye was fixed was closed in by the great white throne.

THE REV SAMUEL MANNING, 1885

WOTTON-UNDER-EDGE – *Hugh Perry's 17th-century gabled almshouses*

THE SHARP escarpment of the Cotswolds looms above the town. It was known locally as 'Woulton-under-Ridge' in the reign of Henry III, when it first began to prosper as a market town and centre for the woollen industry. The long river valleys cutting into the Edge provided motive power for several water mills. Only a very few survive, and most have been converted or adapted for other uses. On the far side of the street are the almshouses bequeathed to the town by the former Sheriff of London Hugh Perry, who held the office in 1632. They were built in 1638 to house six poor men and six poor women of the town. A central domed cupola surmounts their six gables, each with its finial. Note the drip moulds above the windows, which direct the rain away from the walls. A central passageway leads to a courtyard and a tiny, beautiful chapel; on the east side of the courtyard are the Dawes almshouses of 1720. In this photograph, the almshouses look in need of some attention; they have been restored in recent years.

Left: WOTTON-UNDER-EDGE, CHURCH STREET 1900   46308

THIS ROUND HOUSE is one of five built along the Thames & Severn Canal – houses like this are only to be found on this particular canal. Each was a house for a lengthsman, responsible for the maintenance of a length of canal, and his family – they collected tolls from passing barges. Some of the Round Houses had upwards conical roofs, but this one had a downward conical roof; it acted as a funnel for rainwater, which was collected in an underground tank. These houses have survived in various states of preservation, and have now been restored by the Cotswolds Canals Trust. Built in the latter half of the 18th century, the canal ran from Inglesham to Stroud, where it joined the Stroudwater Navigation to the River Severn at Framilode.

Right: LECHLADE, THE ROUND HOUSE C1955   L147036

LECHLADE – *The Round House, canal lengthsman's home*

BIBURY – *Arlington Row, from simple barn to cottage homes for 17th-century weavers*

THE RIVER COLN played an essential role in Bibury's development. From Saxon times it provided the motive power for local corn and cloth mills, in addition to feeding the local system of water meadows, which were made fertile by regular flooding. Bibury is a well-spread-out settlement. This is because it was formed from a number of tiny hamlets and individual properties that gradually grew together over the centuries. Arlington Row is one of the most picturesque – and most photographed – rows of warm Cotswold stone cottages in the Cotswolds. Its first function was a barn. Then in the 17th century the building was converted into home workers' cottages for weavers in the wool trade. Traditionally, weavers' cottages had stable doors; the top half was left open so that passing traders could see the quality of the work in progress. Arlington Row is now owned by the National Trust.

Above:
BIBURY,
ARLINGTON ROW
C1960   B530002

Right:
BIBURY,
ARLINGTON ROW
C1960   B530024

CHELTENHAM – *Elegant Regency terraces in a fashionable spa town*

THREE CENTURIES ago, Cheltenham was another stone village on the edge of the Cotswolds. Its fortunes changed in 1715 when a mineral spring was discovered. Within a few years, fashionable society had begun to arrive to take the waters, and Cheltenham changed its character from a small country town to a leading spa and health resort. The town quickly became a retirement home for military officers and colonial administrators, who occupied the spreading Regency terraces along the Promenade. It is interesting to compare the Promenade, purposely designed for Cheltenham's newer role, with the High Street. The latter is narrow in comparison with the Promenade, its road space given over to the passage of vehicles rather than of pedestrians. The opposite is true with the design of the Promenade; here the pavements are much wider than the roads, allowing residents and visitors to walk in safety away from traffic, which was contained in narrow carriageways. Similarly, the cream-white houses and buildings in avenues such as the Promenade are much more spacious and elegant than the original dwellings and lodging places in the High Street. It was for the building of the Promenade and the surrounding crescents and terraces that many of the quarries were opened in the neighbouring hills. It is possible to calculate the dates of Cheltenham's terraces by comparing the architectural styles. The early terraces, such as Royal Crescent, lack the adornment of some of the later buildings; they have iron railings around their balconies instead of stone archways and colonnades.

Left: CHELTENHAM, THE PROMENADE 1901   47261P

Above: CHELTENHAM, THE MEMORIAL GARDENS 1937   87922

HIGH TOWN (right) is still the main shopping area in Hereford. In medieval times, people coming to trade in Hereford quickly set up a market in an open area just outside the city walls. There may well have been an ulterior motive here, for by trading outside the town these people probably thereby avoided paying the tolls that were due from traders once they were within the safety of the walls. Much revenue was probably lost as a result of this, and so it was not long before the city walls were extended to enclose the market area that we now know as High Town. It was once known as the Butchery, where meat was sold. The Old House, a three-storey timber-framed structure, was built in 1621 by John Able, the king's carpenter, the year after the Pilgrim Fathers sailed on the Mayflower. It was once one of a row of houses extending out into the middle of High Town. At one time the building was a branch of the Worcester City and County Bank, which was later taken over by Lloyds Bank. It was Lloyds that gave the building to the city in 1928; it was then converted into a museum.

LEDBURY – *Narrow cobbled lane of jettied houses*

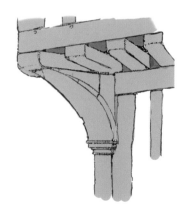

LEDBURY has a strong poetic tradition which, according to some, dates from William Langland in the 14th century. It is debatable whether he was connected with the town. But the links with Elizabeth Barrett Browning and John Masefield cannot be denied: Masefield was born here, and Elizabeth Barrett Browning lived at Hope End, just north of Ledbury, as a child and young woman, and wrote her first poetry here. The Dymock poets (Rupert Brooke, Edward Thomas, Robert Frost and others) lived and worked near Ledbury too. This narrow cobbled street is always appearing in period dramas on film and television. A painted room was recently discovered in one of the timber houses here – the painting dates from around 1560, and had survived beneath layers of later plastering and wallpaper.

Left: LEDBURY, CHURCH LANE 1938 L132004

Right: HEREFORD, HIGH TOWN 1891 29285P

Above: A TYPICAL OVERHANGING JETTY, BUILT AS A PLATFORM ON THE STOREY BELOW

HEREFORD – *The Old House, built in 1621 by John Able, the king's carpenter*

It is truly an old mean built and very dirty city, lying low, and on the banks of the Wye, which sometimes incommodes them very much by the violent freshes that come down from the mountains of Wales.

DANIEL DEFOE,
'A TOUR THROUGH THE WHOLE ISLAND OF GREAT BRITAIN'
1724-27

WEOBLEY – *The Ley, exceptional 16th-century farmhouse, framed with massive oak timbers*

THIS is widely considered to be one of the most beautiful houses in the entire county of Herefordshire. It dates from 1589 and was built as a farmhouse, the year after the Spanish Armada attacked England; with its eight gables, it has probably changed very little, in outward appearance at least, since that time. Its oak timbers have never been painted to achieve the black and white effect, which was a popular Victorian idea – compare this house with The Old House in photograph 29285 (page 81). This picturesque and placid scene is enhanced by the perfect image of the house reflected in the still water.

Above: WEOBLEY, THE LEY C1960   W304132

WEOBLEY – *Ancient black and white houses on the Black and White Village Trail*

WEOBLEY, south-west of Leominster, is one of the finest medieval villages in England, and is on the Black and White Village Trail. Some of the cottages date back to the 14th century, and so does the Red Lion Inn, which we see beyond the cottage in the foreground. This cottage is a wonderful example of cruck construction: two pairs of timbers were set up, each pair slightly curved and formed from the split halves of the same tree trunk. The crucks met at the apex and supported a horizontal ridge-pole which carried the rafters; the crucks were supported by lateral tie-beams. Vertical walls and thus more internal space were formed by lengthening the tie-beams, on which horizontal wall-plates rested, and by upright posts rising from the foot of the crucks.

Right: WEOBLEY,
CRUCK COTTAGE C1955   W304101

BROMYARD – *Lower Brockhampton*

LOWER BROCKHAMPTON manor house was built between 1380 and 1400 for John Domulton, descendant of the Brockhampton family. The manor house stands in a steep wooded valley in the Welsh Marches; in those troubled times defence was essential, hence the moat, which is bridged by a small detached jettied 15th-century gatehouse. The manor house is set back from the moat, and faces south across a grassy court. The building is L-shaped, and the great hall, open to the rafters, is attached to the two-storey east wing; the massive timbers came from the estate. The family's great chamber is on the first floor, and huge red brick chimneys rise up from the end walls. In the mid 18th century a descendant of the family had a new house, Brockhampton Court, built a mile to the south to replace the old-fashioned manor house. Lower Brockhampton, one of the most romantic and picturesque half-timbered buildings in the Welsh Marches, was left to sleep undisturbed. It is now in the care of the National Trust.

Left: BROMYARD,
LOWER BROCKHAMPTON C1955   B229089

LEOMINSTER – *Simple street of small traders*

PRONOUNCED LEMSTER, this is the second town in Herefordshire. Today, with all our 'mod cons', we never pause to consider the problems of looking clean. Both ladies in this picture are wearing white aprons, and even the little girls have clean pinnies on – yet all these will have been washed by hand. This was doubtless a street of small traders and workers. A milliner and dressmaker are both listed as residents in the 19th century. Like so many timber-framed houses, which were built without substantial foundations, this one appears to have moved and settled over the years thanks to the timbers distorting and twisting.

Left: LEOMINSTER, VICARAGE STREET 1906　55492P

The town has a remarkably clean and respectable appearance; the streets are good, abounding with shops containing all the comforts and necessaries of life. There are many houses bearing the semblance of great antiquity, being ornamented with a variety of figures and devices, carved of wood, many of which are still in a high state of preservation, and many through the despoiling hand of time much defaced.　E C LASCELLES, 'DIRECTORY OF HEREFORDSHIRE', 1851

STOURPORT-ON-SEVERN – *Cave dwellings*

STOURPORT stands where the River Stour meets the Severn; it grew in importance after James Brindley built a canal junction there in the 1760s. The meeting of all these waterways proved important in the industrial development of the region. The rivers and canal are used for pleasure boating these days. The soft rock cliffs at Redstone Rock above the Severn south of Stourport led to the creation of many caves. Some people believe that these are rock shelters carved out in prehistoric times. There are many legends of witches living in the caves, which indicate that they may well have been pagan sacred sites, and some of the caves were used by hermits in medieval times. Some of these were enlarged and used as dwellings until quite recently. They are now the haunt of visitors strolling out from the nearby towns.

Right: STOURPORT-ON-SEVERN, THE ROCK CAVES 1931　84630

BROADWAY – *Neglect brings rapid deterioration and decay to this old farmhouse*

FROM about 1600 Broadway was a thriving staging post, and horse-drawn carriages by the dozen stopped here to feed and water en route from London to Worcester – a journey of more than 17 hours. Over 30 inns offered passengers refreshment and accommodation. More (and many say the best) asparagus is grown here than anywhere else in the country – locals call it 'gras'. This tumbledown cottage shows the reality of cottage life in the 19th century, far removed from the romantic and immaculately honed restorations that we see today. Its decline must have been rapid and sudden for the inhabitants: a photograph by George Washington Wilson shows the house just a few years before Frith's photograph, and there are few signs of serious decay, with only a little wear on the thatch.

Today, Broadway gives the appearance of great prosperity, and attracts thousands of visitors. With its handsome houses in honey-hued stone, its village green shaded by spreading chestnuts, its oak-beamed inns offering foaming pints of ale, it is the quintessential English village.

Above: BROADWAY, CHINA SQUARE 1899   44117

WORCESTER – *A 16th-century building, here converted to a dairy and workshop*

WORCESTER is a city of elegant buildings, though a number were lost in the 20th century. But many more were restored and preserved so that we might enjoy them today. Wonderfully ornate signwriting indicates that Mr Charles Collins, a Victorian builder, had his offices in this house in the Cornmarket, while a naïve painting of a cow above the right-hand window advertises a dairy. A carved inscription above the left-hand lower window reads 'Love God WB 1577 RD Honor Kinge'. Since the photograph was taken an inscription has been painted above the right-hand window, reading 'Ye Olde Kinge Charles House'. This has led many to believe that this is the house from which Charles II so famously escaped after the Battle of Worcester, running out of the back door (which led to the city walls) as his pursuers came in at the front. However, that King Charles House is round the corner on New Street. But it does bear the same date –1577 – so perhaps both were part of the same building. Today the house has a third storey, but this has in no way detracted from its charm.

Above: WORCESTER, OLD HOUSE IN THE CORNMARKET C1890 W141508P

LUDLOW – *An ornately-carved facade created for a 17th-century lawyer*

IT IS generally agreed by those outside the profession that lawyers charge too much. This large, grand and ornately ornamented house is the evidence. It was built by a lawyer, Rees Jones, in the early 1600s. By the end of the century it had become an inn with stabling for 100 horses. Today the decorative carving is much as it was when first built, with the exception of the balconies, which were added in the 19th century. The main room on the middle floor on the left has a truly magnificent plaster ceiling. The house is described by Nikolaus Pevsner as 'that prodigy of timber framed houses'. The name of the hotel is derived from the ostrich feather carvings on the three gables; ostrich feathers are the badge of the Prince of Wales, and the house was built just after celebrations in 1616 at the investiture of the future King Charles I as Prince of Wales. The Feathers remained an inn for the next 200 years, and was occasionally the scene of cock-fighting and prize-fighting. Candidates for parliamentary elections would make speeches from the hotel balcony, then invite voters inside for a drink to help secure their votes.

The streets are lined with many quaint old houses, decorated with various devices, moulded in plaster, and set within crossing timbers of black oak. The town has an antique stamp, and suggests a prosperity that has in great measure passed away. VICTORIAN GUIDE, C1890

Above: LUDLOW, THE FEATHERS HOTEL 1892 30829P

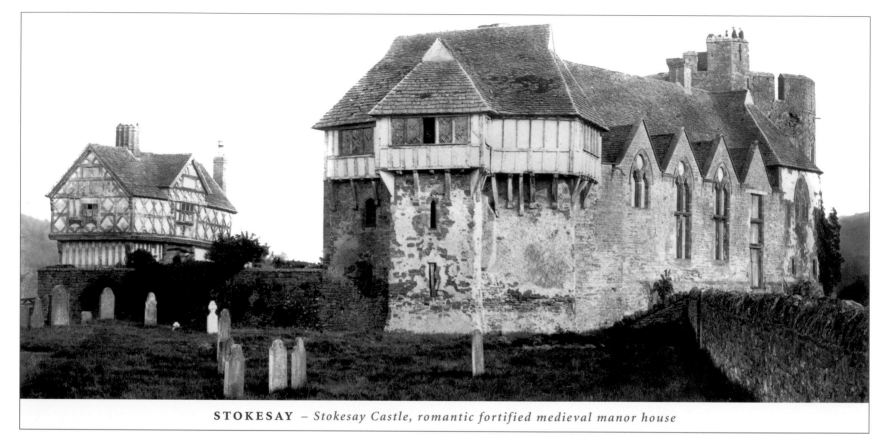

STOKESAY – *Stokesay Castle, romantic fortified medieval manor house*

STOKESAY CASTLE has to be one of the most romantic medieval sites in the country. It is, in fact, a fortified manor house – one of the two battlemented towers can just be glimpsed to the far right in the photograph above. It was built at the end of the 1200s by Lawrence de Ludlow, a wealthy wool merchant; at that time England's wealth lay in its wool.

In the 1600s Stokesay was owned by Lord Craven. He fell in love with Elizabeth of Bohemia (sister to Charles I); rumour has it that they secretly married after the death of her husband, Frederick of Hanover. Lord Craven refurbished Stokesay for Elizabeth; it is sad to think that she never came here as she died of the plague in 1662. It stands in a bad defensive position, however, so that when it was attacked during the Civil War the defenders wisely abandoned it and took refuge in the church instead. As a result it fortunately survived the war.

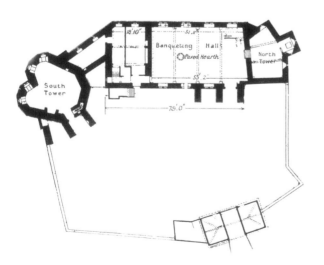

Above: STOKESAY, STOKESAY CASTLE FROM THE CHURCHYARD C1865 2239

Right: STOKESAY, STOKESAY CASTLE, A ROOM IN THE NORTH TOWER 1910   62491

The view from the churchyard, at the brink of the river-cliff, is a very striking one. Deep below, almost at the foot of the precipice, lie the river and the lower town, and on the opposite side the banks of the valley again rise steeply, as usual green with grass and thickly clad with trees. These, after a while, give place to bare rock, a fine crag overhanging the sward on the left bank of the Severn, and adding greatly to the charm of the scene.

VICTORIAN GUIDEBOOK, C1890

BRIDGNORTH – *The Hermitage, Saxon cave dwelling above the River Severn*

THE TOWN and castle of Bridgnorth sit on a cliff of the very soft red sandstone typical of this part of the county. The 'glue' that holds the grains of stone together is nothing more than rust, iron oxide, which gives the stone its bright red colour. Over the years dwellings were carved out within the stone; the caves at Bridgnorth are thought to be of Saxon (AD 597-1066) origin, and some were occupied into the 20th century. The Hermitage lies in ruins now, destroyed by the passage of time and, it is said, by the fires of its temporary occupants, the homeless poor.

Above: BRIDGNORTH, THE HERMITAGE 1896   38136

STRATFORD-UPON-AVON – *William Shakespeare's birthplace before and after restoration*

STRATFORD-UPON-AVON is where William Shakespeare was born in April 1564, and it is the most visited place in England apart from London. William was in fact lucky to survive; within a few weeks of his birth Stratford was struck by an outbreak of plague, and between 30 June and 31 December there were 238 recorded deaths. Around the town, doors were marked with red crosses and daubed with the words 'Lord have mercy on us.'

Restoration work on Shakespeare's birthplace in Henley Street began in 1857, and just how extensive it was can be seen by comparing S21601 with S21602, taken about ten years later. It was really two houses, one for the family and the other where John Shakespeare, William's father, worked as a glover and wool merchant. The restoration was directed at bringing the appearance of the property into line with the earliest known illustration of it; the buildings either side were demolished to reduce risks from fire. Since Shakespeare's day the house had gone through a number of incarnations: the family home became a butcher's shop, and the other part became an inn. The restorers were lucky in that the timber framework, stone floors, cellars, and several internal walls were original, dating from the early 16th century.

Above left:
STRATFORD-UPON-AVON, SHAKESPEARE'S BIRTHPLACE C1850
S21601

Below left:
STRATFORD-UPON-AVON, SHAKESPEARE'S BIRTHPLACE 1861
S21602

By the 1890s around a quarter of the visitors to Shakespeare's birthplace were Americans. Many guidebooks stated that the house contained 'more or less authentic' relics of Shakespeare. One Victorian guidebook reported that 'the relics are evidently imported: an ancient bedstead, old-fashioned chairs, and the like; interesting in their way, but with nothing to tell us of the poet. He remains to the most zealous relic-hunter as great a mystery as Homer himself'. Today the west part of the house is furnished in a late 16th- to early 17th-century style appropriate to a comfortably-off family. Note the old desk in the fireplace.

Above left: STRATFORD-UPON-AVON, SHAKESPEARE'S BIRTHPLACE 1892 31063

Below left: STRATFORD-UPON-AVON, SHAKESPEARE'S BIRTHPLACE 1892 31062

It has been greatly – perhaps over-much – restored; but extensive repairs were absolutely necessary, and all sorts of excrescences – fungoid growths, as it were, of plaster, wood and brickwork – had to be removed. A narrow, awkward staircase leads to the upper floor, where, in a small, low room overlooking the street, he was born. It is now almost unfurnished. The walls are covered with graffiti, where clown and peer, fool and genius, shoulder one another.

VICTORIAN GUIDEBOOK, C1890

COMPTON WYNYATES – *Mellow 15th-century manor house set in magnificent topiary garden*

THIS CHARMING, romantic country house was built between 1480 and 1520 on the site of a Norman manor house. Much of the mellow stone came from the ruined Fulbrook Castle, which had been given to William de Compton by Henry VIII; the stone combines beautifully with brick and timber. It lost its moat after the Civil War. Henry VIII slept here, and tucked away under the roof is a room with three exits; it was used to hide a priest, and contains an altar carved with crosses. By the 19th century, the house was an uninhabitable ruin, but restoration began about 1835. The famous topiary garden was laid out in 1895, and at the same time a water garden was constructed on the site of the moat. Picture-book perfection is the keynote at Compton Wynyates. The setting, a quiet hollow tucked away beneath Edge Hill, is as beautiful as the house, which belongs to the Marquis of Northampton.

But of Compton Wynyates I despair of giving any coherent or adequate account. It belongs to the Marquis of Northampton, and it stands empty all the year round. It sits on the grass at the bottom of a wooden hollow, and the glades of a superb old park go wandering upward away from it. When I came out in front of the house from a short and steep but stately avenue I said to myself that here surely we had arrived at the farthest limits of what ivy-smothered brick-work and weather-beaten gables, conscious old windows and clustered mossy roofs can accomplish for the eye. It is impossible to imagine a more finished picture. And its air of solitude and delicate decay – of having been dropped into its grassy hollow as an ancient jewel is deposited upon a cushion, and being shut in from the world and back into the past by its circling woods – all this drives the impression well home. The house is not large, as great houses go, and it sits, as I have said, upon the grass, without even a flagging or a footpath to conduct you from the point where the avenue stops to the beautiful sculptured doorway which admits you into the small, quaint inner court. HENRY JAMES, 1877

Left: COMPTON WYNYATES, THE HOUSE AND THE GARDEN 1922 72098

BROOM – *William Shakespeare's 'Beggarly Broom'*

THERE are a number of 16th- and 17th-century half-timbered cottages in this photograph, but judging by the state of some of them the village was living up to the 'Beggarly Broom' name given to it by William Shakespeare in the verse he is said to have written to celebrate a drinking competition: 'Piping Pebworth, Dancing Marston, Haunted Hillboro', Hungry Grafton, Dudging Exhall, Papist Wixford, Beggarly Broom and Drunken Bidford.'

Left: BROOM, THE VILLAGE 1901   47346

ONLY a couple of miles from Kettering, the village of Barton Seagrave retains plenty of charm and character. These delightful ironstone cottages stand in the lee of the trees; nearby lies Barton Hall, reputed to have been built with stones from a 14th-century castle here. Barton Hall was constructed during the reign of Queen Elizabeth I, and Northamptonshire's most famous historian, John Bridges, was born here in 1666. In this photograph, the thatch is threadbare, but the brick chimneys look relatively new. A later 1960s photograph in the Frith archive shows the cottages rethatched and thoroughly spruced up.

Right: BARTON SEAGRAVE, OLD COTTAGES C1955 B700012

BARTON SEAGRAVE – *Ironstone cottages with threadbare thatch*

The hall has been modernised, and ruined! The two staircases are to be admired for their ponderous oak-timber and carving. The beauty of the house is the great drawing-room, up one pair of stairs, I called King William's room, from the visit he made here. Now, as the windows of this room have been lately glazed in good ancient taste, why was the gallery, the present library, to be defaced by modern sashes? In this house, and in almost every house I ever entered, the first comfort of life is wanting, viz., beds: fine, wide, comfortable beds! I declare I never see them and have never slept in one like my own – smooth, deeply mattressed and six feet wide. I, a poor man, have enjoyed this greatest luxury these twenty-seven years.

JOHN BYNG, 1793 ('RIDES ROUND BRITAIN', EDITED D ADAMSON, FOLIO SOCIETY)

NORTHAMPTON – *Castle Ashby, magnificent Elizabethan house with impressive inscription along its parapet*

THIS MAGNIFICENT HOUSE with its soaring towers and decorative balustrades is situated at the heart of a 10,000-acre working estate surrounded by 200 acres of parkland landscaped by Capability Brown. Its avenues were planted following a visit by William III. The lands at Castle Ashby were given to the Compton family in 1512 by Henry VIII; 62 years later Queen Elizabeth I permitted William, 1st Lord Compton (later the Earl of Northampton) to demolish the derelict 13th-century castle and replace it with the present house. It was finished in 1635; the south wing is attributed to Inigo Jones. Like other houses of its date, it was built in the shape of the letter E. The vast galleried Great Hall is supreme. It is two storeys high with a Gothic timbered roof, and it is dominated by a superb Elizabethan fireplace with oak carvings. On the exterior of the house, running along the topmost parapet, is a carved Latin inscription: 'Nisi dominus aedificaverit domum in vanum laboraverunt qui aedificant eam; nisi dominus custodierit domum frustra vigilat qui custodit eam'. This is a quotation from Psalm 126: 'Unless the Lord build the house, they labour in vain that build it. Unless the Lord keep the house, he watcheth in vain that keepeth it'.

Above: CASTLE ASHBY 1922 72221

QUENIBOROUGH – *Cruck cottage*

ALTHOUGH QUENIBOROUGH is now virtually a part of the outer edge of suburban Leicester, this photograph presents an almost chocolate-box view of this conservation village. The thatched cruck cottage, the museum-piece petrol pump, and the amazing interlocking of roofs, lead the eye inexorably to the needle-like 175-foot spire which crowns the pink granite tower of St Mary's Church; this spire is said by Pevsner to be one of the finest in Leicestershire. The main street is wide, with a fine collection of houses of various dates, styles and materials.

Left: QUENIBOROUGH, THE VILLAGE AND ST MARY'S CHURCH C1955 Q12001

ASFORDBY – *An archetypal country rectory, built in red brick in the early 19th century*

THIS WONDERFUL photograph could be used to illustrate any romantic 19th-century novel. Asfordby lies in the beautiful Wreake Valley, three miles west of Melton Mowbray. In 1564, there were 48 families in the village; today the population is about 2,700. In 1796, the village was described as 'large, having an excellent road made through it'. The lord of the manor at that time was the Rev Thomas Beaumont Burnaby, who was also the rector. He provided John Nichols with much information for his 'History of Leicestershire'. He married Catherine Clark, 'a lady of property', and he built this very spacious, comfortable red brick rectory in about 1810. The older part of the village, including a manor house, the medieval village cross, the rectory, and two old inns is clustered round the 13th-century Church of All Saints.

Left: ASFORDBY, ALL SAINTS' CHURCH AND RECTORY C1955 A211009

NEAR GRANTHAM – *Belvoir Castle, Gothic-style great house, built and rebuilt from Norman times to the 19th century*

THE NAME Belvoir means 'beautiful view', and indeed the castle is visible for miles around, beautifully situated on a spur rising 200 feet high between Nottinghamshire and Lincolnshire. The original Norman castle was rebuilt during the 16th century. Ruinous again by 1649, it was rebuilt by Philip Webb, a pupil of Inigo Jones, and in 1801, James Wyatt remodelled the building; this remodelling had to be completed by the Reverend Sir John Thoroton after fire partially destroyed the new work in 1816, after Wyatt's death. Faced in yellow ironstone, this fairytale composition is the ideal castle of 19th-century romantic fiction, with its towers and crenellations breathing life into the Gothic fantasy world. The aerial photograph shows an apparently unstructured plan, but the castle is in fact roughly rectangular around a central courtyard. On the right-hand side of the building is the Regent's Gallery, transformed by Wyatt from the earlier long gallery, and to the left is the Elizabeth Saloon, named after the 5th Duchess of Rutland. Outside the thick wooded cover, the more open land of the deer park is corrugated by the medieval ridge and furrow of open cultivation.

The classic view below of the castle contrasts the delicacy of the chapel, with its triple Gothic windows and pinnacled octagonal towers, with the somewhat more robust Windsor-like tower to its left.

My arrival at this stately castle was a fiasco. The Duchess [of Rutland] had forgotten that she had told me to come to their little station of Redmile, and when I arrived at that desolate place, with deep snow on the ground and night fast closing in, there was nothing to meet me. The station-master sent his little boy to the next village, and in an hour he returned with an open wagonette, agonisingly cold across the open plain. But I was repaid when we entered the still loveliness of the ice-laden woods, every bough sparkling in the moonlight like crystallised silver; and still more when we emerged upon the plateau at the top of the hill, and the mighty towers of the castle rose pale grey into the clear air, looking down into the wooded frost-bound gorges like the palace of the ice-queen.

AUGUSTUS HARE, 1893

Top: BELVOIR CASTLE, FROM THE AIR C1960   B633078

Above: BELVOIR CASTLE, FROM THE NORTH-WEST 1890   27861

NOTTINGHAM – *Wollaton Hall, spectacular stately home compared to a crystal palace*

WOLLATON HALL is a stunning Tudor building, designed by Robert Smythson and completed in 1588 for the wealthy coal baron Sir Francis Willoughby. The house is built on a high hill overlooking all the surrounding area. There is supposed to be a ghost here: strange lights have been seen in the dovecote, near the stable yard. Cornelius Brown, in his 'History of Nottinghamshire' (1896), describes the house thus: 'Wollaton Hall is one of the stateliest homes of which old England can boast, and the wooded park, where browse the frighted deer, surrounds it with all the beauties of nature … The hall [is] described as "a combination of elegance and art" … It is a crystal palace, combining lightness and grace with imposing stability, and the beauty of its design can best be illustrated by the fact that Sir Joseph Paxton found nothing comparable to it in England … This splendid Elizabethan mansion, as the inscription testifies, took eight years in its completion, and cost £80,000 – an enormous sum in those days. The Ancaster stone used in its construction was supplied in exchange for coal from the pits on the Wollaton estate. The interior of the noble building is no less attractive than its exterior, and its wealth of artistic adornment includes the masterpieces of Giordano, Vandyck, Snyders, Hemskirk, Teniers, Rubens, and others'. Wollaton was eventually sold to the Corporation of Nottingham in 1924; it now contains a natural history museum.

Above: WOLLATON HALL 1928 81579

NEWARK – *The Governor's Old House*

THIS FAMOUS 16th-century timber-framed house, with its three jettied or projecting storeys, was the residence of Richard Willis, the Royalist Governor during the Civil War. Prince Rupert, Charles I's dashing cavalry commander, stayed here in October 1645 after quarrelling with his uncle, the king. Today, the deep gilded glass shop signs have been removed, revealing more of the black timbers. Thomas M Blagg, in his 'Guide to the Antiquities of Newark' (1910), describes the house thus: 'A little further on from the Clinton Arms, at the entrance to Stodman Street, stands a timber-fronted house with overhanging storeys, nicely coved. This was the Governor's house at the time of the sieges of the town during the Civil Wars, when Newark was held for the King under Sir John Henderson, Sir Richard Byron, Sir Richard Willis, and the Lord Bellasis successively. If the visitor walks up the passage marked "Hardy's Yard" at the end of this house, he will be pleased with the long wing running out at the back, with its steep-pitched gable. The old white-washed yard is a favourite subject with local artists'. In this photograph, the roof looks brand new, but there are two broken panes in the top right-hand window.

Left: NEWARK-ON-TRENT,
THE GOVERNOR'S OLD HOUSE 1909 61804P

A straggling, gloomy, depressive, partially-inhabited place the Abbey was. Those rooms, however, which had been fitted up for residence were so comfortably appointed, glowing with crimson hangings and cheerful with capacious fires, that one soon lost the melancholy feeling of being domiciled in an extensive ruin.

WILLIAM HARNESS (ONE OF BYRON'S FRIENDS)

NEWSTEAD ABBEY – *Once a medieval monastery, and ruinous home of the poet Lord Byron*

NEWSTEAD ABBEY was founded around 1170. After the Dissolution of the Monasteries, it was granted to the poet Lord Byron's ancestor, Sir John Byron, in 1539. The Byron family retained the medieval monastic character of the building, which endures to this day. When the poet inherited Newstead, it was extremely dilapidated. He could not afford to repair it, and only furnished a few of the smaller rooms. Byron cleared the Great Hall and the Great Dining Room and used them for fencing, boxing and pistol shooting. He brought his pets – they included a bear, large dogs, and tortoises. He lived here off and on until just before he was married in 1814. Financial pressures meant that he had to sell Newstead; finally, in 1818 his schoolfriend Thomas Wildman bought it. Wildman, who had inherited a fortune, was able to repair and restore Newstead; after his death, the house was bought by William Frederick Webb, a friend of Dr David Livingstone. Eventually, the house came into the hands of the philanthropist Sir Julien Cahn, and he gave it to Nottingham Corporation in 1931.

Above: NEWSTEAD ABBEY, FROM THE WEST 1890 22856

SOUTHWELL – *The Bishop's Manor, a Jacobean-style house built in the ruins of the medieval Bishop's Palace*

Above: SOUTHWELL, THE MINSTER AND THE BISHOP'S MANOR 1920   69456

SOUTHWELL owes its existence to the great minster church that dominates the centre. Not only does this wonderful, mainly Norman collegiate church (a cathedral since 1884) occupy the south-east corner of the town, but clergy houses line the north-east and south-west corners. It is truly a 'company town', with the townsfolk crammed into the north-west corner with their market place at the Burgage. Southwell has also expanded least around its historic core, and is the quietest and least-altered of Nottinghamshire's towns. The Bishop's Manor, nestling in the lee of the minster, was built into the ruins of the 14th-century Bishop's Palace in 1907. Built in a pleasant Jacobean style, it blends seamlessly with the ancient stonework. It occupies the western half of the former palace, and the rest is open to the sky and used as a walled garden. The former palace was largely destroyed at the end of the Civil War after King Charles I surrendered in Southwell in 1646. Cornelius Brown, in his 'History of Nottinghamshire' (1896), reports: 'Subsequently the town was occupied by Puritan troops, and it is said that the nave of the minster was used as a stable for their horses. The palace was damaged, and the unrestrained troopers wrought havoc at their own sweet will. "From this time," says Mr. Shilton, "ravage was the order of the day, and Cavaliers, Roundheads, and Covenanters alternately exercised their several abilities with such effect that when, soon after the surrender of Charles, an order was made for dismantling the palace very little was found undone". '

HARLOW – *The picturesque thatched Round House*

THE QUIRKY Round House was built about 1750 on the London Road just north of Maypole Corner, near the site of Potter Street's famous Prentice Pottery, which produced England's first ceramic dish. It was a two-up, two-down cottage, and given the large thatched roof and tree trunk supports, was probably designed more for effect than convenience. It was demolished in 1955 when that area of Harlow New Town was being developed. There is an existing example of this kind of house in Finchingfield.

Above: HARLOW, THE ROUND HOUSE, LATTON STREET C1950 H22020

SOUTH WEALD – *Queen Mary's Chapel*

THIS 16TH-CENTURY lodge, set in what was the walled kitchen garden of Weald Hall, has unsubstantiated associations with (pre-Bloody) Queen Mary. The story is that she stayed here and observed Mass in the 1540s, whilst still a princess. A document of the 1840s tells how 'after the suppression the property remained for a time in the crown; and at the Hall during that period dwelt the princess afterwards Queen Mary; her name has left many a legend lingering about the dwelling; and yonder little looking antique detached gardeners' house was the Roman Catholic chapel in which she worshipped ... The park [is] studded with long rows and clustering clumps of noble trees, which probably stood here when Queen Mary wandered in their midst'. The brick chapel is built in English bond (one row of bricks laid lengthways, one row laid head-on), and has carved brick ornamental finials on every gable. Weald Hall itself was demolished in 1950.

Left: SOUTH WEALD, QUEEN MARY'S CHAPEL 1906 54457

Below: TIPTREE, MESSING MAYPOLE MILL C1955 T116021

TIPTREE – *Messing Maypole Mill*

TIPTREE HEATH was once 'a miserable barren piece of land' haunted by tinkers, squatters, and horse-racing fans. In 1775 a brick tower-mill was built to extremely high standards near the crossroads by John Matchett, a Colchester millwright. It was modernised in the late 19th century. Though it stopped work in 1920, it still looked smart in the 1950s with its black cap, finial ball and lightning conductor. It has now been converted into a house, and is surrounded by a modern housing estate.

LAYER MARNEY – *The Towers, magnificent Tudor gatehouse to a mansion that was never built*

THIS MAGNIFICENT eight-storey gatehouse was built by Sir Henry, 1st Lord Marney, in the 1520s. The rest of the mansion he had planned was never built: Sir Henry died in 1523, and the Marney family died out two years later. During the Great Earthquake of 1884 the building was severely damaged; soon afterwards, a report in The Builder magazine stated that 'the outlay needed to restore the towers to anything like a sound and habitable condition would be so large that the chance of the work ever being done appears remote indeed'. However, brother and sister Alfred and Kezia Peache decided to repair the building. They re-floored and re-roofed the gatehouse, and also laid out the garden to the south of the Towers. The Towers are admired for their sheer scale, and for the terracotta ornamentation on their parapets.

ABOVE: LAYER MARNEY, THE TOWERS 1892   31548

JAYWICK – *Much-loved simple bungalow homes of pioneer plotlanders*

Above: JAYWICK, 'B' TYPE BUNGALOW C1955 J4027P

THE FARMLAND that became Jaywick was originally sold off after the agricultural depression of the late 1920s. Chalets – intended as holiday-homes only – were built on the available plots. Colin Ward, in his paper 'The Hidden History of Housing' (published on the website History and Policy), explains that the Essex plotlands were on the heavy clay known to farmers as 'three-horse land', which was the first to go out of cultivation in the agricultural depression; other plotlands grew up on vulnerable coastal sites like Jaywick Sands and Canvey Island. The local council felt that the area was unsuited to permanent development, but by the 1950s Jaywick was well established. By that time, the plotlanders wanted their holiday homes to stay in the family and eventually to become their retirement home. These bungalows might appear small and jerry-built, but to their owners they were full of happy holiday memories. Colin Ward adds that 'the plotlands tended to be upgraded over time. Extensions, the addition of bathrooms, partial or total rebuilding, the provision of mains services and the making-up of roads are part of the continuous improvement process in any old settlement'. Also, the original settlers were remarkable for their 'defensive independence and their strong community bonds. The residents of Jaywick Sands, for example, had for decades organised a service for emptying Elsan closets, known locally as the 'Bisto Kids', until, after fifty years, a sewer was built.'

Left: JAYWICK C1955 J4041

EAST ANGLIA – *Decorative plaster pargetting*

PLASTERING, and decorative plastering, or pargetting, is a traditional finish for cottages and houses in East Anglia. The old plaster was usually made of lime, sand, bullocks' hair, and cow dung, carefully mixed and matured for a long time; it made a finish as tough as leather. Sometimes the plaster was combed or pricked into traditional pargetting patterns; on grander houses, the pargetting could be extremely elaborate, as we see here.

Crown House (below) started life as the King's Head. It was a late 16th-century building that underwent a makeover in 1692: this was when the shell-hood was added to the doorway, the pargetting executed, and the pub's name changed to the Crown. There is no substance to the myth that Nell Gwynn ever lived here.

In the view of a building in Saffron Walden (below left) we see pargetting with birds and plants on the projecting gable, and in the centre to the left of the drainpipe it is just possible to pick out the shape of a single leg. This is almost certainly a trade sign, and as the toes are showing it is possibly that of a corn cutter, the early name for a chiropodist. Over the archway are two life-size figures, Tom Hickathrift and the Wisbech Giant, who both occur in East Anglian legends. There is a date further along in the highest gable, 1676; this is not the date of the building, but the date of the pargetting. This explains why the figures are in 17th-century costume.

In Ipswich's Buttermarket is the town's most famous house, the Ancient House (opposite right). Also known as Sparrowe's House, this remarkable jettied building is over five hundred years old. Its interest lies in the elaborate moulded plasterwork designs on its outer walls – it is probably the best surviving example of pargetting in Britain. It was around 1670 that Robert Sparrowe remodelled the building, with the pargetting reflecting his interest in the known world at that time – the four continents of Europe, Africa, Asia and America are represented in the panels below the first-floor windows. The arms of Charles II (who, it is said, hid here after the Battle of Worcester) are over the main doorway.

Top left: SAFFRON WALDEN, THE OLD SUN INN C1955 S43039

Above left: SAFFRON WALDEN, THE OLD SUN INN C1955 S43040 (DETAIL)

Right: NEWPORT, CROWN HOUSE 1932 85127

Opposite right: IPSWICH, THE ANCIENT HOUSE 1921 70398P

KERSEY – *Brick, timber and plaster combine in a harmonious village street scene*

Few villages, and those by no means pretty; but no appearance of poverty. The houses, indeed, poor enough on the outside – but the casements in good repair – the floors clean – and the people with decent working-clothes on, and healthy looks. No beggars at all to be seen. The roads, made of pounded flint, are hard and smooth – the horses fly along. It is certainly a pleasurable sensation to be thus transported with ease and swiftness, and without fatigue or exertions – a lazy sort of selfish pleasure, however, which one feels almost ashamed of enjoying.

LOUIS SIMOND, 'IN RURAL SUFFOLK', 1810

PHOTOGRAPH K136042 (above) typifies the unforgettable appeal of Kersey: brick, timber and plastered houses are raised to allow for the slope, with higher and higher steps to the front doors, and there is a pleasing variety of roof levels, gables and window shapes.

Photograph K136027 (opposite above), looking from the church towards the water-splash of the Brett, shows a very different regard for timber-framed buildings compared to today. However, thanks to the falling plaster on the house on the left, we can see the laths beneath. Laths are pieces of timber (battens) nailed up to the timber framing, forming the foundation structure of the outer coat of plaster, which is trowelled over the laths. As the plaster is pushed up against the laths, it oozes through the gaps between them and flops over; when the plaster sets, this 'mechanical bond' prevents it from falling down. Traditional plaster was made up of lime, sand and horse or bullocks' hair. The hair fibres helped to bind the mixture together.

ALDEBURGH – *The 'Ionia', houseboat and holiday home*

FRESTON – *Freston Tower, England's oldest folly*

THE 'IONIA' was a wooden fishing smack built in Grimsby in 1872 and set up on the Slaughden saltings as a houseboat. It has in its time even been a holiday home for orphan girls. By the mid 1960s its parlous state was giving concern, and it was destroyed by fire in 1974.

Opposite: KERSEY, THE STREET C1965 K136042

Top: KERSEY, THE VILLAGE C1955 K136027

Above: ALDEBURGH, THE OLD 'IONIA' 1952 A28001P

Above right: FRESTON, THE TOWER 1893 32233

FRESTON TOWER was built in 1578 by Thomas Gooding, a rich Ipswich merchant. It is arguably the oldest folly in the country. Looking out over the River Orwell, it can be found in the village of Freston, south of Ipswich. Samuel Tymms, writing in 1856, says: 'Freston Tower is a striking and pleasing feature in the picturesque scenery of the Orwell. It is built of red brick, is quadrangular in form, and in plan about 10 feet by 12, and is crowned by an open arcaded parapet ... It is six storeys high, and has as many rooms, one on each storey; the communication therewith being by a winding staircase occupying the east or principal face of the tower. The principal room was on the fifth storey ... The windows are square with pointed pediments, and are very small, except in the state chamber, which has three windows of three lights each. The ascent to the leads is by an elegant turret at one of the angles. There is but one fireplace on the second floor, but this has no chimney, and appears to have been a later construction ... Freston Tower was used as a receptacle for persons afflicted with the small pox from 1772 to 1779, by Mr Buck, an eminent surgeon at Ipswich.' Today, thanks to the Landmark Trust, who painstakingly restored it, it is possible to stay in Freston Tower for a while.

THORPENESS – *The House in the Clouds, a cunningly disguised water tank*

THORPENESS, a purpose-built seaside village in the tiny hamlet of Thorpe in Aldringham, was built between 1910 and 1928 as a 'Garden Village and model holiday hamlet by the sea' by Glencairn Stuart Ogilvie, a Scottish landowner, playwright and barrister. The village was built round an artificial lake, the Meare, and had a Peter Pan theme. Around the Meare were imitation lath and plaster houses (actually made of concrete), and cottages that looked like a medieval gatehouse. When the village was built there was no mains water, so a water tower was needed. Ogilvie built a five-storey house with a 30,000-gallon water tank on the top. The tank was disguised with a pitched roof, chimneys and mock windows. The building was originally known as the Gazebo. Mr and Mrs Malcolm Mason moved into the house below the tank, and Mrs Mason loved it. She wrote poems for children, and one, inspired by her house, was called 'The House in the Clouds': 'The fairies really own this house – or so the children say. In fact, they all of them moved in upon the self same day'. When she recited this to Ogilvie, he was enchanted, and exclaimed: 'The name must be changed to The House in the Clouds!'. Thorpeness is now on mains water; the huge tank in the House in the Clouds has been dismantled, and the house is a holiday cottage. The most elegant post mill, originally a corn grinding mill, used to stand in nearby Aldringham. It was moved in 1923 to serve a different purpose – to pump water to the huge tank.

Left: THORPENESS, THE HOUSE IN THE CLOUDS AND THE WINDMILL
C1955 T38012

SOMERLEYTON was built between 1844 and 1851 by Sir Samuel Morton Peto, the railway contractor, builder, and developer of Lowestoft. The building was designed by John Thomas, who had worked with Peto on the new Houses of Parliament, in the Jacobean style, incorporating the existing house. Pevsner described Somerleyton Hall as 'more Jacobean than any original Jacobean house'. The Winter Garden was a miniature Crystal Palace, 126 feet by 136 feet, with glazed arcades and a domed glass roof. The fountain and statue in the fernery (28729, centre) was made by Joseph Durham in 1868. Under-floor heating allowed tropical and exotic plants to be grown in beds, whilst climbing greenery smothered the pillars and roof. Most of the structure was demolished in 1914, but a small section and some statues survive.

Left: SOMERLEYTON, SOMERLEYTON HALL 1891
28726

Opposite: SOMERLEYTON, SOMERLEYTON HALL,
THE WINTER GARDEN 1891 28729

SOMERLEYTON – *Somerleyton Hall, a sumptuous Victorian country house in the Jacobean style*

GREAT YARMOUTH – *The Rows, narrow alleyways of tightly-packed fishermen's cottages*

A row is a long narrow lane or alley, quite straight, or as nearly so as may be, with houses on each side, both of which you can sometimes touch at once with the finger-tips of each hand, by stretching out your arms to their full extent. Now and then the houses overhang and even touch above your head, converting the row, so far, into a sort of tunnel, or tubular passage. Many and many a picturesque old bit of domestic architecture is to be hunted up amongst the rows. In some rows there is little more than a blank wall for the boundary. In others, the houses retreat into tiny courts, where washing and clear-starching were done, and wonderful nasturtiums and scarlet-runners are reared from green boxes.
CHARLES DICKENS

THE ROWS made up a pattern of narrow streets unique to Great Yarmouth, running parallel from east to west between the Market Place and King Street on one side, and the Quays on the other. They were so narrow that goods had to be transported along them on special horse-drawn carts called trolls. The writer Charles Dickens was fascinated by Great Yarmouth, and describes the Rows very well (see above right).

There were over 150 rows originally, but bomb damage in both world wars has reduced that number by over a half. In 1898 it was estimated that 12,000 people lived in the Rows: about a third of the living-rooms received an hour's sunlight, the others no sunlight at all. By 1911 the Borough Engineer, J W Cockrill, had paved or concreted the surface of every Row: as a consequence he acquired the nickname of 'Concrete Cockrill'!

Above left: GREAT YARMOUTH, ROW NUMBER 60 1908   60654

SALHOUSE – *Norfolk reed growing, stacked and used as thatch*

THIS WONDERFUL PICTURE shows Norfolk reeds in all stages of their growth and use: growing in the water, gathered into boats, and bundled and piled up to await transport further afield. A partially-thatched hut on the right of the picture, with a beautifully thatched cottage behind and another example of fine thatching on the building at the left, show the ultimate use of nature's gift. Reeds grow along the banks of the broad. Of all the materials used for thatching, reed is the most durable – it can last up to a hundred years. At the roof ridge, reed thatch is sometimes given a cap of sedge over the top for weatherproofing.

Above left: SALHOUSE, THE BROAD 1902   48147

WROXHAM – *Bure Court*

OFTEN CALLED the Capital of the Broads, Wroxham is the largest village between Norwich and Yarmouth. On a dull day this large broad can appear a threatening expanse of rough, grey water, but it provides opportunities for excellent sailing. This is a typical example of many luxury homes built in the first half of the 20th century which enabled their owners to enjoy life beside the water. The roof is thatched with local reed, and the principal rooms are elevated to avoid floods and to afford excellent views of the waterways. An interesting balcony has steps down to the garden, where leisure furniture and croquet hoops indicate a relaxed way of life. A motor launch is tied up at the private mooring.

Right: WROXHAM, BURE COURT C1940   W156109

EAST DEREHAM – *Bishop Bonner's Cottage, decorated with fish-scale pargetting*

NOTICE the splendid running frieze of pargetting along the front of the cottage (dated 1502 in the wreath at the point of the gable), and notice too the varying states of repair of the cottage over the years. We may be thankful that it has been saved from the somewhat dilapidated state it was in in 1898, but does it look just a little too perfect in the 1960s photograph opposite?

Note how the pargetting has been painstakingly modelled to resemble fish-scale tilehanging. Bishop Bonner was rector of East Dereham from 1534 to 1538, and this building, situated near the church, was his house. Bonner was much hated for his role in the burning of 'heretics' at the stake; he was Bishop of London under Queen Mary, 'Bloody Mary', and was instructed by her to show zeal in promoting the Catholic faith.

East Dereham is said to get its name from a miracle of St Withburga in the 8th century: during a famine, two deer appeared in answer to her prayers to give their milk to the nuns in the nunnery she had founded.

Opposite left: EAST DEREHAM,
BISHOP BONNER'S COTTAGE 1898 42765

Above: DETAIL FROM 42765

Left: EAST DEREHAM,
BISHOP BONNER'S COTTAGE C1965 D25043

HINGHAM – *Dignified Georgian houses facing the village green*

HINGHAM is situated in Breckland, a very prosperous area from medieval times onwards. These handsome 18th-century houses (from left to right Quorn House, Little London and Admiral's House) are good examples of the attractive houses which abound in this small town. A village sign by Harry Carter dominates the green. Hingham was responsible for providing New England with many settlers in the 17th century, where they founded another Hingham. Abraham Lincoln's ancestors came from here, and there is a bust of him in the aisle of the parish church.

Above: HINGHAM, MARKET PLACE C1955 H309014P

SANDRINGHAM – *The Entrance Lodge, a tour de force of carefully clipped creeper*

THIS EXQUISITE royal estate was purchased by Queen Victoria for the Royal Family in 1861. Within its 7,000 acres are the lands of seven parishes, and a profusion of woods, sandy heathland and broad grassy rides, which are the haunt of deer. Under the neatly-trimmed ivy and bushes is the entrance lodge to Sandringham House and gardens (above), which were subsequently opened to the public in the early 1900s.

Above: SANDRINGHAM,
THE ENTRANCE LODGE 1896   38401

Right: SANDRINGHAM,
THE DUKE OF YORK'S LODGE 1896   38399

Left: QUEEN VICTORIA C1890   F6505

CLEY-NEXT-THE-SEA – *A perfect example of East Anglian brick and flint cottage building*

THIS PICTURESQUE flint village was once the most significant of the Glaven estuary ports, and its old Custom House bears testimony to its prestigious past. Silting of the waterway presaged the decline of Cley's influence, and coastal vessels now pass it by. It has become a centre for holiday visitors, and many of its lovely brick and flint cottages have been painstakingly restored as holiday lets. The windmill, too, is a holiday retreat today.

STANDING on the fringes of the Norfolk marshes, Blakeney, like Cley (see above), once knew busier days. Its capacious natural harbour, protected from the sea by the long spit of sand, Blakeney Point, attracted coastal trading vessels until the early years of this century. The landscape offers birdwatchers an irresistible mixture of dunes, saltings, mudflats and creeks. The town is studded with fine brick and flint houses with steep pantiled roofs. Flint is a remarkably hard and durable building material, and was much used in districts where no other stone is available, particularly Norfolk (and in the chalk districts of the southern counties). It could be used as rubble masonry, as here, and the quoins and dressings were of brick. The typical Norfolk roof of red pantiles suits the flint walls well. In East Anglia, flint cottages were sometimes colour-washed, or even coated with tar.

Above: CLEY-NEXT-THE-SEA, THE WINDMILL 1955 C118010

Right: BLAKENEY, THE VILLAGE 1925 77527

BLAKENEY – *Harmonious street scene with brick and flint and pantiles*

ST IVES – *Overcote Ferry, a classic cottage fireside*

THIS APPEARS to be a very old cottage, but at this date it looks more luxurious than it would have been when it was built. The floor is brick, with a rush mat on top (it would originally have been beaten earth), and there is plenty of well-made and well-polished furniture, while a fine 8-day country-style long case clock (probably made c1800) ticks patiently in the corner. Knick-knacks and ornaments are displayed round the walls and on the mantelshelf, including a grinning Toby jug, candlesticks, and calendars, and a mirror hangs on the wall beside the clock. Note how dark this room is – it has tiny windows and no electric light, just like all cottages of this type. The chief feature of the room, of course, is the fireplace; it was originally a huge inglenook fireplace, but at some point a central hearth has been raised and enclosed with bricks and cement and whitewashed. A salt box hangs to the right of the fireplace. The bellows will soon set the logs in the hearth ablaze, and we can sit down by the fire and enjoy the hot toddy waiting on the table.

Left: ST IVES,
OVERCOTE FERRY, THE FIRESIDE INTERIOR 1914

HOUGHTON – *Timber framing and mansard roofs seen half a century apart*

THE ABOVE photographs of Houghton show the St Ives Road. In the photograph on the left is a row of three houses with their original front doors; further down the street are two 18th-century mansard-roofed cottages, one of which is thatched. At the end of the street is Manor Farm.

The later photograph on the right shows Manor Farm after the plaster had been removed from the timber frame, and we also see those 18th-century mansard-roofed cottages more closely. The farmhouse has some lovely details on its timber frame and some original pargetting; the small oriel window at the gable end was blocked when a modern chimney was built into an end room.

Above left: HOUGHTON, THE VILLAGE 1914   66962
Above right: HOUGHTON, THE VILLAGE C1960   H464004

LINCOLN – *Rhythmic classicism contrasts with medieval irregularity*

LINCOLN, the county town of Lincolnshire, is situated where the limestone ridge is cut through by the River Witham. The great medieval minster church dominates the city and the countryside for miles around. Reaching the top of Steep Hill, we are looking west from Exchequer Gate, the medieval gatehouse into the cathedral close, towards the castle gatehouse. The three-gabled and jettied timber-framed building of 1543 on the right was restored in 1929 and is now a tourist information centre. It contrasts with the fine Georgian sash-windowed building beyond – what an interesting juxtaposition. Note that the Georgian architect has made no attempt to echo the lines of the older building next door. By the 1950s, much of the plaster on the wall facing the motor car in the top photograph had been removed, (see left), revealing more of the timber work, but the charming 18th-century many-paned bow window is still in place.

Above: LINCOLN, CASTLE HILL 1906 55115AP

Left: LINCOLN, BAILGATE C1955 L49064

NOW the headquarters of the Society for Lincolnshire History and Archaeology, the Jew's House dates from the 1170s, and is one of the oldest houses in England. It was indeed once owned by a Jewess, Belaset, in the 1280s. At the rear is Jew's Court, where, it is said, little St Hugh of Lincoln was crucified by Jews in 1255: all utter nonsense, of course. The Jew's House is one of Lincoln's surviving early medieval stone houses; the city has more than most. It was a merchant's house, with shops on the ground floor and the hall and chamber on the upper floor; the hall was heated by a stone fireplace above the doorway. Two windows with elaborately carved and moulded arches light the rooms of the first floor.

Left: LINCOLN, THE JEW'S HOUSE 1890   25664P

Above: LINCOLN, THE JEW'S HOUSE C1950   L49017

CHESTER – *Stanley Palace, an ornately decorated Elizabethan town house*

STANLEY PALACE, formerly called Derby House, stands on or near the site previously occupied by the Dominican friars. Built in 1591 for Sir Peter Warburton, a lawyer and MP for Chester, this fine town house passed into the hands of the Stanley family. The long, low, two-storey house is unusual in that its principal front is at right angles to the street. It is gabled and ornately decorated, designed in the Elizabethan manner with finials on the gables, large leaded casement windows on both floors, carved and patterned woodwork, and plaster panels. The interior has a long oak beamed hall; from it a grand oak stair leads to the gallery. Each storey has a good 18th-century room west of the stair. It is said that there are two ghosts here: a grey lady, and James Stanley, 7th Earl of Derby, who was held here in his town house before his execution in 1651. In 1866 the house was threatened with being dismantled and taken to America. It was saved by the Chester Archaeological Society. In 1928 the Earl of Derby presented the Corporation with Stanley Palace, and it was restored (the smaller wing facing the street was reconstructed in 1935). Note the profusion of urns, statuary, cannons, and architectural carving – was there a museum here?

Chester is still an antique town, and mediaeval England sits bravely under her gables. Every third house is a 'specimen' – gabled and latticed, timbered and carved, and wearing its years more or less lightly. These ancient dwellings present every shade and degree of historical colour and expression. Some are dark with neglect and deformity, and the horizontal slit admitting light into the lurking Row seems to collapse on its dislocated props like a pair of toothless old jaws. Others stand there square-shouldered and sturdy, with their beams painted and straightened, their plaster whitewashed, their carvings polished.   HENRY JAMES, 1872

Left: CHESTER, STANLEY PALACE 1923   73867

CONGLETON – *Moreton Old Hall, moated manor house*

MORETON OLD HALL is known as Little Moreton Hall today. Standing two miles south of Congleton, the magnificent moated manor house, now owned by the National Trust, was originally built in the mid 15th century by Sir Richard de Moreton and added to by successive generations of his family. As with many houses of this period, it has a secret room; the difference at Little Moreton is that a second secret room exists beneath the moat. The house also has a central cobbled courtyard, a long wainscoted gallery, a chapel and a great hall, all very fine examples of their kind. Spiral staircases connect the floors. The long gallery twists and teeters, for it was built without foundations. The formal knot garden is laid out in typical 17th-century style, and herbs and vegetables familiar at that time are still grown there. Its survival in its near-original form probably owes much to the fact that its owners were often very stretched for cash and could never therefore afford to alter it, add to it or change it in any way – how fortunate for us today. In the 19th century, it was lived in by a farmer together with his animals, and the chapel was used as a coal cellar.

Above: CONGLETON, MORETON OLD HALL 1902   48670

We drove out to Eaton Hall, the seat of the Duke of Westminster, the many-millioned lord of a good part of London. It is a palace, high-roofed, marble-columned, vast, magnificent, everything but homelike, and perhaps homelike to persons born and bred in such edifices. A painter like Paul Veronese finds a palace like this not too grand for his banqueting scenes. But to those who live, as most of us do, in houses of moderate dimensions, snug, comfortable, which the owner's presence fills sufficiently, leaving room for a few visitors, a vast marble palace is disheartening and uninviting.   OLIVER WENDELL HOLMES, 1887

CHESTER – *Eaton Hall, grand Victorian Gothic ducal seat*

OUTSIDE CHESTER stands Eaton Hall, seat of the Duke of Westminster. The Eaton Hall we see in the photograph was designed by Alfred Waterhouse in grand Victorian Gothic style between 1869 and 1882. The ornamental gardens were laid out by William Porden. The hall and estate even had its own railway – the 15-inch gauge line was based on that developed by Sir Arthur Heywood at Duffield Bank near Derby. The house was used as a hospital in both world wars, and the Royal Naval College moved here from Dartmouth during the Second World War; the house then became an Officer Cadet Training School until 1960. Much of Waterhouse's hall and the railway have been demolished.

Above: EATON HALL 1914 67528P

BUXTON – *Elegant 18th-century spa town with graceful crescents and domes*

BUXTON is one of only two spas in Britain where hot springs bubble to the surface. This classic view of Buxton from The Slopes was taken during its heyday as an inland spa created largely by the efforts of the 5th Duke of Devonshire. In the centre is the magnificent 154-foot diameter dome of the Great Stables and Riding School, at the time the largest unsupported dome in the world, while to the right in the background is the Palace Hotel. In the right foreground is Buxton's famous Crescent, built for the 5th Duke of Devonshire between 1780 and 1784 by John Carr. It was constructed from locally-quarried gritstone, and has 42 pilasters and 378 windows. It is said to have been modelled on the Royal Crescent at Bath. However, not everyone was impressed: the 18th-century traveller John Byng thought Buxton highly unsatisfactory – see his comments below. The crescent was recently renovated, and is being converted into a spa hotel. To the left are the Natural Baths and the Old Hall Hotel.

In the photograph below left we see Broadwalk, with the entrance to the Pavilion Gardens on the left. Broadwalk was originally known as Cavendish Terrace; development began in the 1860s, and it soon became a fashionable place to live or take rooms.

A most uncomfortable, dreary place; and the Grand Crescent might be better named the Devonshire Infirmary. Snug lodging-houses, with adjoining small stables, were more necessary and comfortable than useless, ill-contrived grandeurs: but the Duke, I suppose, was made prey of by some architect.

JOHN BYNG, 1790
('RIDES ROUND BRITAIN',
EDITED D ADAMSON, FOLIO SOCIETY)

Above: BUXTON,
THE VIEW FROM THE SLOPES 1932 85213

Left: BUXTON, BROADWALK 1914 67575

BAKEWELL – *Haddon Hall, 'the most romantic and complete medieval manor house in England'*

OFTEN DESCRIBED as 'the most romantic and complete medieval manor house in England', Haddon Hall, the Derbyshire home of the Manners family, the Dukes of Rutland, stands on its limestone bluff overlooking the River Wye, three miles south of Bakewell.

The present building mainly dates from the rebuilding of the Norman castle by Sir Richard Vernon in the 14th century, with additions from the 15th and 16th centuries. Haddon Hall remains today much as it was then; no changes were made to the house in later centuries, because after the dukedom of Rutland was conferred on the family in 1703, they moved to Belvoir Castle, and Haddon lay untouched for over 200 years. Then in the 1920s the 9th Duke and Duchess of Rutland restored the house and gardens, and once again made it habitable. In the interesting early photograph below, a formally-dressed Victorian group pose

decorously in the porch of the entrance to the banqueting hall. Note the Vernon and Manners crests carved above the doorway, the square-profile lead rainwater pipes, and the neatly-trimmed box hedges on the right.

View 5236 (opposite) shows the most modern room in the house – it dates from the 16th century! Haddon's oak-panelled long gallery was used by the family to take exercise when the weather was bad. It is 110ft long by 17ft wide, and the frieze above the panelling incorporates both the peacock of the Manners family and the boar's head of the Vernons.

Haddon was the scene of Dorothy Vernon's elopement with John Manners, the son of the Earl of Rutland – it is thanks to her that the house belongs to the Manners family. Other fine rooms in the house include the splendid medieval kitchens and banqueting hall.

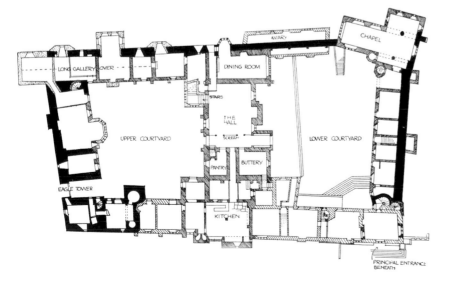

The twilight deepened, the ragged battlements and the low, broad oriels glanced duskily from the foliage, the rooks wheeled and clamoured in the glowing sky; and if there had been a ghost on the premises I certainly ought to have seen it. In fact I did see it, as we see ghosts nowadays. I felt the incommunicable spirit of the scene with the last, right intensity. The old life, the old manners, the old figures seemed present again.

HENRY JAMES, 1872

Above: HADDON HALL, THE LONG GALLERY C1870   5236
Opposite left: HADDON HALL, THE COURTYARD C1870   5232P

BONSALL, VIA GELLIA – *Tufa Cottage, a picturesque hermitage folly*

A WOMAN poses in her horse-drawn trap outside Tufa Cottage, on the Via Gellia road from Cromford to Bonsall (above). The cottage was constructed entirely from blocks of tufa, a rough, thick, lightweight rock-like calcium carbonate deposit formed by lime-rich water in this limestone country. The massive rough-faced blocks give the cottage the air of a picturesque hermitage folly. The Via Gellia runs through a steep-sided narrow wooded valley; it was named after Philip Gell of Hopton Hall, Cromford, who had it built in the late 18th century. He wanted to improve access between the Gell family lead mines at Carsington and the smelter at Cromford – lead mining was still very much a local industry in the area at that time.

Above: BONSALL, VIA GELLIA, TUFA COTTAGE 1886   18586

Left: BONSALL, VIA GELLIA, TUFA COTTAGE 1892   31298

Above: EYAM, THE VILLAGE, NORTH END 1896 37812

Below: EYAM, THE PLAGUE COTTAGES 1910 69211P

THE VILLAGE of Eyam found itself a place in the history books thanks to the sacrifice made by its inhabitants during the Great Plague of 1665-66. When the plague reached Eyam in a consignment of cloth from London, the villagers, encouraged by their vicar William Mompesson, decided to isolate themselves from the outside world in an attempt to contain the outbreak. Though the disease abated during the winter months, it returned with a vengeance in 1666. In all, 257 villagers died. Some of the plague victims were buried outside the churchyard, possibly in an attempt to stop infection within the community. The seven members of the Hancock family were interred in a walled enclosure near to Riley House Farm. The twin-gabled cottages in photograph 69211 (below) are where the infamous plague first struck in 1665. These are substantial cottages, sturdily built in coursed rubble with stone dressings; note the unusual windows, which slide horizontally to open and shut. We can see the tower of the parish church of St Lawrence in the background, where the vicar led the sacrifice – his own wife died in 1666 and is buried in the churchyard. An interesting statistic is that during the 20th century, plague has killed 18 million people worldwide.

EYAM – *The terraced cottages where the great plague of 1665 first struck*

BOLTON – *Hall i' th the Wood, where Samuel Crompton developed his spinning mule*

ALTHOUGH no longer 'i'th wood', this wonderful building is still full of character. Begun in 1483 by Lawrence Brownlow, owner of a fulling-mill, the half-timbered hall house was extended by his descendants. After the Civil War it was extended again by Alexander Norris, and subsequently rented out to various tenants, among them young Samuel Crompton and his parents.

In 1799 Samuel Crompton developed his spinning mule here, which revolutionised the cotton industry, and now a museum in the house charts the development of textile manufacture. This is thanks to Lord Leverhulme, who bought the Hall when it had fallen into disrepair; he paid for its restoration, and gave it to Bolton in 1902.

Above: BOLTON, HALL I'TH WOOD 1894   34389

CHORLEY – *Lord Leverhulme's pigeon tower*

THIS STRANGE building, standing on the edge of the moor above Rivington village, is a pigeon tower and summerhouse. It was erected in 1910 for Lord Leverhulme, the son of a Bolton grocer, whose fortune came from the manufacture of Sunlight Soap. He bought the estate in 1899 and later donated much of it to Bolton Corporation. The top room, used by Lady Lever, gave her marvellous views all around, while ornamental doves and pigeons were kept in the two bottom floors. Behind the tower Lord Leverhulme built a large bungalow, which was burnt to the ground when a suffragette, campaigning for votes for women, set fire to it. Undeterred, he built another one on the same site. Its gardens are now overgrown, and the bungalow itself has disappeared.

Above: RIVINGTON,
THE ROAD TO RIVINGTON PIKE C1960   C537009

NEAR BOLTON – *Turton Tower, ancient pele tower and farmhouse*

TURTON TOWER lies four miles north-east of Bolton. It is basically two buildings, a pele tower dating from the 1100s, modernised around 1450, and a farm house or family hall, added in the late 14th century. This photograph clearly shows the interesting mix of building styles, from the Dutch gable on the right to the sturdy pele tower on the left. This is a wonderful example of the way that houses were expanded piecemeal as circumstances dictated.

Pele towers were unique to the north of England, constructed as a defence against the marauding Scots. They were small, square or oblong, and built of stone, with very thick walls. Designed to withstand short sieges, they usually had three floors. The windowless ground floor was used for storage and for keeping animals; the first floor was the hall and kitchen; and the top floor was used for living and sleeping. From the flat battlemented roof it was possible to keep a look out, and to fire at raiders. In the 17th century, Turton Tower was the home of Sir Humphrey Chetham, founder of Chetham's Hospital and Chetham's Music School in Manchester. James Kay lived here in Victorian times; the Manchester to Bolton railway was built through his estate, and he demanded that the railway bridges be decorated with battlemented towers so as to blend in with the medieval ambience. The house is now a museum.

Above: TURTON TOWER 1897   40106

BURNLEY – *Towneley Hall*

TOWNELEY HALL was first opened to the people of Burnley as a public park and art gallery on 20 May 1903. The opening ceremony was performed by the Earl of Roseberry. Like many old houses, Towneley has developed over hundreds of years. Some parts of the south-east wing go back to the 14th century, yet the other side dates from c1600. The clock over the entrance has been marking the passing of time for about 350 years. Richard Towneley re-built the central great hall in 1725. The original front of the building dated from c1500, but in 1700 it was removed and used for additions to the north-west wing. The family crest, a sparrowhawk, can be found in many places around the building. The two diamonds in Towneley's crown are the chapel and its carved altarpiece – the room is constructed entirely of oak. This is the only place in England where you can gaze upon the vestments of an abbot made in c1400, and marvel at the stitching and sewing from 600 years ago.

Left: BURNLEY, TOWNELEY HALL 1906 54201

Above: BURNLEY, TOWNELEY HALL 1906 54202

HEYSHAM – *Mrs Kellett's cottage tearoom*

LYING CLOSE to the larger holiday centre of Morecambe, close by the broad bay, Heysham has been popular with visitors since the Victorian period, many coming to sample the famous locally brewed non-alcoholic nettle beer. In consequence, several of the ancient cottages opened their doors as tea rooms and cafes, offering lunches and high teas with home-made cakes and biscuits. Kindly-looking Mrs Kellett stands at her door – let's hope that she has just baked a fresh batch of scones! On the left, a date stone reads 1633 with the initials TC and EC, almost certainly celebrating a marriage.

Left: HEYSHAM, COSY CORNER C1900   H81301

SALTAIRE – *Titus Salt's philanthropic creation: a model village for his mill workers*

I have visited some of the most filthy and wretched abodes that the mind of man can conceive, in which misery of the lowest description was personified …there are scores of wretched hovels, unfurnished and unventilated, damp, filthy in the extreme and surrounded by stagnant pools of human excrement and every thing offensive and disgusting to 'sight and smell'. No sewers, no drainage, no ventilation. Nothing to be seen but squalid wretchedness on every side, and the features of the inmates show a perfect and unmistakable index of their condition; all this is to be seen in the centre of this wealthy emporium of the worsted trade.

THE BRADFORD OBSERVER, 1845

TITUS SALT (1803–76) was a woollen cloth manufacturer in Bradford, and made his fortune by being the first to weave alpaca. In his day the population of Bradford had grown vastly and rapidly, and the living conditions for the workers in the mills were atrocious. The Bradford Observer of 16 October 1845 reported the dreadful plight of the cloth workers (see quotation above right).

Salt's Victorian idealism led him to believe that a happy, healthy and fulfilled workforce was a productive workforce; his plan was to build an industrial plant on an unprecedented scale on the banks of the Aire, and along with the mill, Salt decided to build a model village to be known as Saltaire.

The local partnership of Lockwood & Mawson was appointed as architects to the Saltaire project, and a leading engineer of the day, William Fairbairn, given the responsibility for the structural design of the mill, which was completed in 1853. The workers' houses were built to a high standard. Starting near the bottom of the valley in 1854, the development progressed uphill. The names given to the streets are a reflection of what Salt held dear – his allegiance to the Crown, his wife and his children. By 1868, Salt had built housing for his workers that was unrivalled at the time. Weekly rents varied from 3s (about 15p) for a standard two-bedroom house, to 5s (25p) for a larger, three-bedroom house with garden. For recreation, Salt laid out a spacious park on the opposite side of the river and canal. Provision was made for welfare benefits, and help was given to the aged, infirm and sick. The Club and Institute, now the Victoria Hall, provided enlightenment and education for the workers and their children. Only two things were missing from this village: a pub and a pawnshop. It was described as 'a paradise on the sylvan banks of the Aire, far from the stench and vice of the industrial city'.

Above: SALTAIRE, VICTORIA ROAD 1893 33187

Below: SALTAIRE, THE MILL AND THE CRICKET PITCH 1888 21024

The only thing in character here is an old ivy tree covering much of the front. Within it is filthy; and without there is a little dirty flower garden, instead of a gloomy thicket of trees.

JOHN BYNG, 1792 ('RIDES ROUND BRITAIN', EDITED D ADAMSON, FOLIO SOCIETY)

KNARESBOROUGH – *St Robert's Chapel, memorial to Robert Flower, a cave-dwelling hermit*

ST ROBERT'S CHAPEL is a cave, which was carved into the rock alongside the River Nidd in the early 15th century in memory of Robert Flower (1116-1218), a hermit who lived in a cave near here. Pilgrims are said to have come from far and wide to visit him, for he was believed to have had a gift for healing; pilgrims also came to receive spiritual guidance, or simply to visit a famed and revered holy man. The somewhat grotesque carving outside the cave represents a knight drawing a sword, and it is said also to be a portrayal of Robert; however, the date of the carving is in some doubt – it may have been made in the 18th century. Next door to the cave is a famous Knaresborough folly known as the House in the Rock. It was completed in 1791, and has four rooms built one on top of the other.

Above: KNARESBOROUGH, THE WAYSIDE CAVE SHRINE, NEAR THE HOUSE IN THE ROCK 1892   30616

AFTER Henry VII became king, Henry Clifford built the living quarters in the Tudor Conduit Court and the Tudor entrance to Skipton Castle – the masons' marks can still be seen here.

Held by the de Clifford family for 375 years, Skipton Castle is best known for its role during the English Civil War, when Sir John Mallory and his 300-strong garrison withstood a Parliamentarian siege that lasted for three years. When the garrison finally surrendered, its stand was recognised by the Parliamentarians, who allowed it to march out with full honours of war, fully armed and with drums beating and colours flying. One of the features of the courtyard is the yew tree, which is still standing and is thought to be more than 300 years old. It is said to have been planted by Lady Anne Clifford – she also erected a stone tablet above the Tudor doorway to celebrate the castle's restoration.

Right: SKIPTON,
THE CASTLE, CONDUIT COURT 1893   33162P

SKIPTON – *Skipton Castle, and Lady Clifford's 300-year-old yew tree*

People live to a great age here, owing to the fine air and good water, and perhaps owing more to their distance from temptation.   JOHN BYNG, 1792 (AT ASKRIGG)

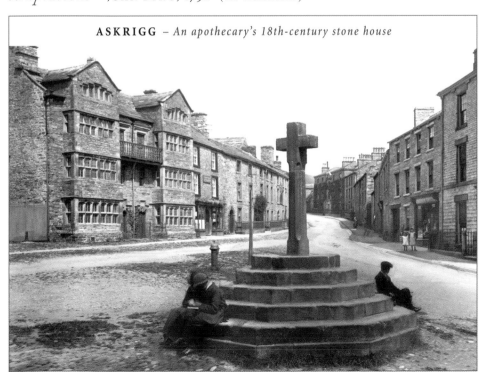

ASKRIGG – *An apothecary's 18th-century stone house*

THE STONE-STEPPED ancient market cross watches over Askrigg's market square as it has for over 500 years. Stately town houses, mainly dating from the 18th century, line the square in this village, which was once the 'capital' of Wensleydale. The grand four-storey house to the left of the cross is the Old Hall, built in 1678 by William Thornton. The Thorntons owned the house until the late 1740s; they installed the balcony on the third floor, and from here they could watch the popular sport of bull-baiting in the market place (the ring to which the bull was tethered is still there today). In 1746 the last of the Thorntons died, and the Old Hall was divided into two. John Addison, a dyer, lived in one half, and James Lightfoot in the other. James Lightfoot was an apothecary; people visited his shop for medicines, but like a modern GP he made home visits. (In 1756 he built himself a new house in the town, now known as the Apothecary's House.) In later years the Old Hall became a private hotel. Sad to say, the Old Hall caught fire in October 1935, and the house was so badly damaged that it had to be pulled down.

Left: ASKRIGG, MARKET CROSS 1911   63468

YORK – *Jettied houses create a timeless medieval atmosphere*

York is an old town, and of course very ugly.

LOUIS SIMOND, 1811 (AN AMERICAN TRAVELLER)

IF WE strip away the Victorian details in this photograph, we are transported back into late medieval times, when these jettied timber-framed houses were occupied by merchants, shopkeepers and also metalworkers, who plied their trade at street level and lived above their commercial premises. Building space was at a premium within the narrow city walls, and plots were consequently small. 'Timber skyscrapers' were a logical solution, each storey being constructed separately and overhanging that below. The houses huddle together, bringing each other significant structural support.

Excavations in the backyards here have discovered medieval hearths and furnaces which were used in the metalworking process, largely for working copper; industry would never be permitted in the centre of a city today, but in medieval times it was common. (The shop fronts we see in this picture are probably Georgian and Victorian; in medieval times there would have been more discreet wooden shutters which folded down to form a counter.) Another custom surviving from medieval times is the large brush trade sign on the left (now in the York Castle Museum – it advertised Seale's Brush and Mat Warehouse); in the Middle Ages hardly anyone could read, so figurative signs had to be used. In the background is a glimpse of one of the towers of the great minster dedicated to St Peter, from which the street got its name.

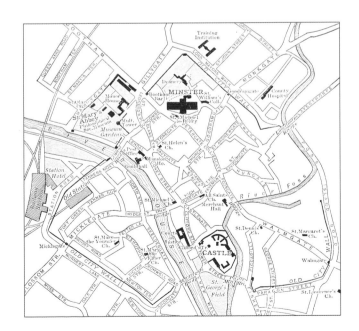

Above: MAP OF YORK C1900
Left: YORK, LOW PETERGATE 1892 30632P

IT is believed that this tiny building was the rectory to one of York's city churches—it was demolished in 1939, and an office block now stands on the site. Here we see it when it operated as a small shop. Its selling space must have been minimal. Shops like this might see no more than a dozen customers a day, and were often run by widows, struggling to pay the rent to the landlord as well as the suppliers' bills.

There is abundance of good company here, and abundance of good families live here, for the sake of the good company and cheap living; a man converses here with all the world as effectually as at London.

DANIEL DEFOE, 1724–27

Left: YORK,
HEMMEN'S SHOP 1909   61864

The houses of the old town – the side away from us, are all red-roofed, and seem piled up one over the other anyhow, like the pictures we see of Nuremberg.

BRAM STOKER, 'DRACULA', 1897
(DESCRIBING WHITBY)

SITUATED in a deep ravine on the estuary of the River Esk, Whitby earned its living from the sea, either by whaling, fishing, coastal trading or shipbuilding. For centuries it was often easier for people coming to or going from Whitby to make their journey by sea rather than attempt to travel overland. Here, in Argument's Yard, the house on the right is derelict, the stone stairs have seen better days and the outside toilet looks ready to collapse. A fisherman's oilskin is slung over the stair rail, and the boy on the right is showing a large fish to his friends – it is part of his father's catch, and they will be having it for supper. This was one of the many narrow yards near the harbour. Here children could play safely, and the fishermen could prepare their nets. Argument's Yard is named not as a result of a quarrel but after a family that once owned property there.

Above: WHITBY, THE HARBOUR 1885   18168
Right: WHITBY,
ARGUMENT'S YARD 1913   66290P

WHITBY – *The shabby charm of the fishermen's quarter*

SANDSEND – *Rugged stone cottages built to withstand sea gales*

SANDSEND is about three miles from Whitby, situated at the mouth of Sandsend Wyke; the village is almost hidden from view because of the mighty cliffs and Mulgrave Wood nearby. In the 12th century, Sandsend was recorded as having 53 tenants' cottages belonging to the lord of the manor. These cottages are typical of this part of the Yorkshire coast. Built of large blocks of rough ashlar laid in courses, they are roofed with pantiles, as are almost all the village houses hereabouts. The roofs are low-pitched to withstand the gales off the sea, and the windows and doors are picked out in bright paint. The area is known as Dunsley Bay, and Sandsend is really two villages. The village reached prosperity in the 17th century with the discovery of alum, which was used in the dying and tanning industry. The alum mines gave employment until 1867, a span of more than 250 years. There are still many traces of the workings of the alum mines nearby.

Left: SANDSEND, THE VILLAGE 1925
77728

BUILT in the late 18th century, this house seems the archetype of the country rectory. How many rectors' daughters have played croquet and flirted with their suitors on the broad lawns? How many rectors' wives have entertained their friends to tea on the terrace? In the years 1825 to 1865, this rectory was home to the Pattison family. Dorothy Wyndlow Pattison was born on 16 January 1832, the eleventh child and tenth daughter of the rector of Hauxwell. After her schooling she wanted to join Florence Nightingale in the Crimea, but her father forbade this. Instead she became a pioneer of civil nursing, spending much of her life in Walsall, where she ran the Cottage Hospital. Her skills were such that she carried out much work normally done by surgeons. She died on Christmas Eve 1878 in Walsall, where a statue commemorates her life. The Rectory, her birthplace, was demolished in 1958.

Right: HAUXWELL, THE RECTORY,
BIRTHPLACE OF SISTER DORA 1913 66039

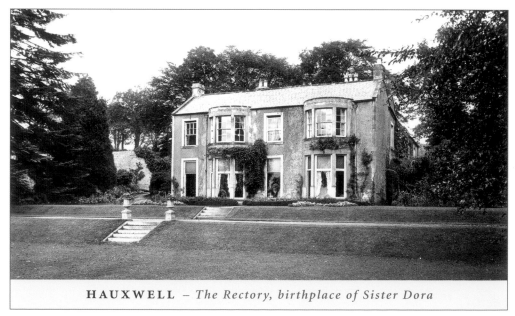

HAUXWELL – *The Rectory, birthplace of Sister Dora*

KENDAL – *A typical yard*

KENDAL was founded on the wealth won from the wool of Lakeland sheep. Its motto is 'Pannis mihi Panis', which means 'wool is my bread'.

But wool was not Kendal's only industry, and other trades, such as rope making, dyeing, and tanning were carried on in the many yards which lead off the main streets. These yards, so characteristic of Kendal, developed from burgage plots running from the main streets. In the yards were cottages (we can see typical examples in the photograph) and workshops. The yards might be named from a feature in them, like Two-Seater Yard in Highgate, where a seat for the weary was placed on each side of the entrance; or from a business, like Post Office Yard; or from the name of a prominent resident. Gates at the heads of the yards were often closed at 10pm, not to keep invaders out, but to keep the residents in. Conditions in the yards were cramped, and good hygiene was virtually impossible.

Each yard would contain a midden, just one earth closet from which the night soil was taken to the river, and just one communal tap – that is, if water was not to be brought from the same source; this produced health hazards, despite the efforts of housewives to keep their homes and families clean and healthy. Disease, especially cholera, took its toll, although there were some who lived to ripe old age.

Today, of course, the yards are charming and picturesque, and this photograph reflects that charm. A lad sits on his handcart on the right; he appears to be in conversation with a friend seated on the other side of the cobbled yard, while others look on as they pose for the camera.

Above: KENDAL, STEELE'S YARD
123 HIGHGATE 1914 67393P

KENDAL – *Levens Hall, a fine Elizabethan mansion with striking topiary gardens*

HAWKSHEAD – *Sturdy dwelling built in the dry masonry method*

THIS HOUSE was home to the poet William Wordsworth, greatest of the Lake Poets, when he lodged here with Ann Tyson whilst he attended Hawkshead Grammar School between 1779 and 1787 following the death of his mother. He carved his name into one of the desks at the school, which can still be seen, and while he was here he wrote his first poem, a commemoration of the school's bicentenary. This cottage dates from the 16th or 17th century. Much of this building seems to have been constructed in the dry masonry method: mortar was seldom used, but stones were often fixed in earth mixed with water but with no lime. Houses built in this way could be plastered or whitewashed, like the central section of the house we see here.

LEVENS HALL, near Kendal, a fine Elizabethan mansion built for the Bagot family around 1580, is constructed around a 14th-century pele tower (a defensive home built at a time when the Scots were making border raids). The magnificent topiary gardens were laid out in the 1690s on the orders of Colonel Grahme, Privy Purse to James II; he used the king's gardener Guillaume Beaumont, who had trained at Versailles under Le Nôtre and had laid out Hampton Court's gardens. The box hedges and the yew topiary creations are still clipped by hand – the process lasts from May to December. Some of the topiary pieces have names, including 'Queen Elizabeth and her Maids of Honour', 'The Judge's Wig', and 'The Jugs of Morocco' – morocco was a potent brew drunk at local festivities.

Above: HAWKSHEAD, ANN TYSON'S HOUSE 1892   30536

Left: LEVENS HALL AND THE GARDENS C1955   L447021P

AMBLESIDE – *The house on the bridge*

EASILY the most famous and most photographed building in Ambleside is Bridge House – it is a popular subject for painters, too, including Turner. This tiny one-up, one-down house was constructed on a bridge over the Stock Beck to escape land tax. It was originally built in the 17th century as a summerhouse and apple-store for Ambleside Hall; later it was used as a weaver's cottage, and it is said that at one time a family with six children lived here in its two rooms. It is now a National Trust Information Centre. The roof is noteworthy: the stone slates are laid in the traditional way with the smallest tiles nearest the ridge, which is constructed with interlocking slates.

HAWKSHEAD is one of the prettiest Lakeland villages; it stands at the head of Esthwaite Water. Bobbin manufacture for the wool and cotton mills of the north of England was once an important industry in the Lake District. The mill at Hawkshead was once a vital part of the village's economy. It is easy to see how this narrow Hawkshead street got its name, as it is paved by flagstones which cover the stream that acted as the water supply for cottagers. Note the large gas lamp on the corner of the slate-hung gable of the house on the left. The overhanging first-floor jetties of the whitewashed houses add to the medieval charm of the village, which is a favourite of the many visitors to the Lake District.

Above: AMBLESIDE, BRIDGE HOUSE 1912   64306
Left: HAWKSHEAD, FLAG STREET 1892   30537

COCKERMOUTH – *The birthplace of Lakeland's most famous poet, William Wordsworth*

ENGLAND'S BEST-KNOWN Romantic poet was born in this Georgian mansion in Cockermouth's Main Street in 1770. Wordsworth's father was steward to Sir James Lowther, and moved to the house in 1766. Pevsner describes it as 'quite a swagger house for such a town'; it is indeed very handsome with its porch, well-proportioned façade and grand gate piers – it was built in 1745 for the High Sheriff of Cumberland. Sir James Lowther bought it in 1761 to serve as accommodation for his steward. The house overlooks the River Derwent, and in 'The Prelude' Wordsworth wonders if the river was a primal influence on him (see quotation opposite).

Above: COCKERMOUTH,
WORDSWORTH'S BIRTHPLACE 1906 54996

Was it for this
That one, the fairest of all rivers, loved
To blend his murmurs with my nurse's song,
And, from his alder shades and rocky falls,
And from his fords and shallows, sent a voice
That flowed along my dreams? For this, didst thou,
O Derwent! winding among grassy holms
Where I was looking on, a babe in arms,
Make ceaseless music that composed my thoughts
To more than infant softness, giving me
Amid the fretful dwellings of mankind
A foretaste, a dim earnest, of the calm
That Nature breathes among the hills and groves?

BUTTERMERE – *A typical remote Lakeland farmhouse, in the shadow of High Stile*

BUTTERMERE takes its name from Old English, and means 'the lake by the dairy pastures' – where the butter is made. The hamlet at the foot of Buttermere in the western Lake District takes its name from the lake; it is still the farming settlement it has always been – despite the mountains all around, there are plenty of flat, fertile pastures between Buttermere and Crummock Water. This long, low farmhouse and barn, surrounded by beautiful trees, looks cosy and secure; but life must often have been hard here in this remote and sometimes harsh environment. The views both from and of the lake itself (about a mile long by 400 yards wide) are stunning.

These dwellings, mostly built, as has been said, of rough unhewn stone, are roofed with slates, which were rudely taken from the quarry before the present art of splitting them was understood, and are, therefore, rough and uneven in their surface, so that both the coverings and sides of the houses have furnished places of rest for the seeds of lichens, mosses, ferns, and flowers. Hence buildings, which in their very form call to mind the processes of Nature, do thus, clothed in part with a vegetable garb, appear to be received into the bosom of the living principle of things, as it acts and exists among the woods and fields; and, by their colour and their shape, affectingly direct the thoughts to that tranquil course of Nature and simplicity, along which the humble-minded inhabitants have, through so many generations, been led. Add the little garden with its shed for bee-hives, its small bed of pot-herbs, and its borders and patches of flowers for Sunday posies, with sometimes a choice few too much prized to be plucked; an orchard of proportioned size; a cheese-press, often supported by some tree near the door; a cluster of embowering sycamores for summer shade; with a tall fir, through which the winds sing when other trees are leafless; the little rill or household spout murmuring in all seasons; – combine these incidents and images together, and you have the representative idea of a mountain-cottage in this country so beautifully formed in itself, and so richly adorned by the hand of nature.

WILLIAM WORDSWORTH, 'GUIDE TO THE LAKES', 1810

Above: BUTTERMERE, HIGH STILE 1889 22065

The city of Durham appears like a confused heap of stones and brick, accumulated so as to cover a mountain, round which a river winds its brawling course. The streets are generally narrow, dark and unpleasant, and many of them impassable in consequence of their declivity.   DANIEL DEFOE, 1724

DURHAM – *The formidable Norman castle soars above humbler houses hugging the banks of the Wear*

DURHAM is still dominated from all viewpoints by its castle and the cathedral. Founded in 1072, Durham Castle is one of the largest Norman castles and one of the grandest Romanesque palaces to survive in England. It was built on the site of a fortress to the orders of William the Conqueror on his return from Scotland in 1072, sited on a peninsula overlooking the River Wear and positioned next to a Benedictine monastery. Waltheof, the Saxon Earl of Northumberland, undertook the building work, but over the years a succession of prince bishops have added important sections to the great building. In the 1930s a huge rescue operation had to be carried out to underpin the subsiding foundations: while the cathedral was built on solid bedrock, the castle was built on less substantial material. Together with the cathedral, the castle is now a World Heritage Site.

Above: DURHAM, FRAMWELLGATE BRIDGE AND THE CASTLE 1892   30739

BISHOP TUNSTALL'S gallery leads from the first landing of the Black Staircase of Durham Castle. The inner wall of this gallery was formerly the outer wall of Bishop Pudsey's hall, and the great round-headed doorway (right) which faces the gallery's largest window was once the principal entrance to the lower part of this 12th-century building.

Right:
DURHAM,
THE CASTLE,
TUNSTALL'S GALLERY
1918   68218

THE COUNT'S HOUSE is associated with a Polish-born count called Joseph Boruwlaski; he was remarkable for many reasons, including the fact that he was only 39 inches tall. Often referred to as the Polish Dwarf or the Little Count, he was an accomplished violinist whose musical talent earned him many notable friends and admirers, including George IV and Marie Antoinette. He died at the grand age of 97, and having established himself as a respected member of Durham society, was buried in the cathedral, where his grave is simply marked 'JB'. Although it is still referred to as the Count's House, this little garden house of the 1820s, built in the style of a Greek Doric temple on the banks of the Wear, is actually a folly built near the site of his home. Sad to say, the Count's House today is just a neglected ruin; its association with a diminutive man who was larger than life in the city's history is now apparently forgotten.

Left: DURHAM, THE COUNT'S HOUSE 1914   67129

THE CHARMING village of Blanchland is situated in a narrow, deep, green vale on the north side of the Derwent, nine miles from Hexham. Its name is derived from Norman French, and means 'the white lands' – this could refer to the white habits of the monks of the abbey that was founded here in 1165. After the Dissolution, the abbey buildings were converted into houses. The Blanchland estate eventually passed into the hands of Lord Crewe, and on his death to the Lord Crewe Trustees, who in 1752 began the restoration and repair of the by now dilapidated village. Thus Blanchland became in effect an 18th-century model village, built on the plan of the monastic buildings and out of their old stone. The houses are grouped round what was the cloister of the abbey and its second courtyard (where there was a silver refinery and a fulling mill, possibly belonging to the abbey), all built out of what remained of the abbey buildings. In the centre of the village is the famous Lord Crewe Arms. Some of this building dates from the 12th century, and some from 17th-century alterations. The ghost of Dorothy Forster, sister to Tom Forster who led the Jacobite uprising in 1715, is said to haunt the hotel to this day. It was Tom and his sister who sold the village to Lord Crewe, Bishop of Durham.

Right: BLANCHLAND, THE VILLAGE C1950 B555045

BLANCHLAND – *18th-century model village built on a monastic site*

SOUTH SHIELDS – *Victorian terraces*

LAYGATE LANE is one of a number of sturdy Victorian terraces in South Shields. Many of them were built speculatively by developers as the town expanded as a result of the coal and alkali industries. Terraces like these can be found all over England. These houses were built for far more prosperous families than the houses we see in Ashington (A224022, page 155). They are much larger, with two main floors of living rooms and bedrooms for the family, basements for kitchen, scullery and coal cellar, and attics for servants' bedrooms. Ornamental stone dressings surround the doors and windows, and smart cast iron railings line the pavement.

Left: SOUTH SHIELDS, LAYGATE LANE 1900 S162001

NEWCASTLE UPON TYNE – *The Sandhill, prosperous merchants' houses of the 16th and 17th centuries*

THE OLDEST part of Newcastle is the Quayside; until the 19th century it was the commercial centre for the northeast. At the Sandhill, some of the oldest remaining houses of the Newcastle Quayside can still be seen. They date from the 16th to the 18th century, and originally belonged to rich merchants. Bessie Surtees' House combines two merchant's houses dating from the 16th and 17th century. They are both remarkably well preserved, and one of the houses is a rare survival of Jacobean domestic architecture, with panelled rooms and elaborate plaster ceilings. On the night of 18 November 1772, Bessie, the daughter of Aubone Surtees, a banker, climbed down a ladder from one of the windows and into the arms of her lover John Scott. The couple then fled across the Scottish border and were married at Blackshiels, Midlothian. Scott later became Lord Chancellor of England. At the time of this photograph, the house had become the warehouse of J W Newton & Co. Bessie Surtees' House is now open to the public and administered by English Heritage.

Left: NEWCASTLE UPON TYNE, THE SANDHILL 1894 N16319

Above: NEWCASTLE UPON TYNE C1890 N16303

… The door [leads] to the narrow front passage, beneath the ceiling of which are lodged masts, spars and sails … The dresser is littered with fishing lines as well as with dry provisions and its proper complement of odd pieces of china. Beneath the table and each of the larger chairs are boots and slippers in various stages of polish or decay. Every jug not in daily use, every pot and vase, and half the many drawers, contain lines, copper nails, sail-thimbles and needles, spare blocks and pulleys, rope ends and twine. But most characteristic of the kitchen (the household teapot excepted) are the navy-blue garments and jerseys, drying along the line and flung over chairs, together with innumerable photographs of Tony and all his kin, the greater number of them in seafaring rig … An untidy room – yes. An undignified room – no. Kitchen; scullery (the scullery proper is cramped and its damp floor bad for the feet); eating room; sitting room; reception room; storeroom; treasure-house; and at times a wash-house, – it is an epitome of the household's activities and a reflection of the family's worldwide seafaring.

STEPHEN REYNOLDS, 'A POOR MAN'S HOUSE', 1908 (LIFE IN A FISHERMAN'S COTTAGE)

CULLERCOATS – *A terrace of tiny one-roomed fishermen's cottages*

A COAL PORT in the 17th century, and a seaside retreat for the well-heeled of Newcastle from the late 19th century onwards, Cullercoats was also a noted fishing port. These small cottages, often built in rows or in squares round a courtyard, are typical of the fishing communities of the northeast. Like these ones, the cottages usually consisted of one room, with one door and one window. Inside, the flagstone or cement floor might be covered with linoleum; a hooky (rag) rug, made by the fisherman's wife, would only be brought out for special occasions. As we can see here from the large chimneys, each tiny cottage had an open fire, which as well as providing heat was often used for cooking as well. A large pot was kept beside the fire for storing hot water. From the doors of these cottages fishwives in their distinctive costume sold their fish. Note the very shallow pitch of the roofs and the protective pebbledash on the walls.

ASHINGTON – *Archetypal terrace*

This photograph is included because it typifies the kind of street found in towns and cities all over England: neat terraces of Victorian or Edwardian artisans' dwellings with a handy shop or two on the corner. This particular town, Ashington, began as a pit village when a coal seam was found in about 1867. Before, it had been little more than a few scattered farmsteads. As the population grew, so did the need for houses, shops, schools and public buildings, and the Ashington Coal Company built 300 houses for pitmen and their families. Here, we can see billboards proclaiming the virtues of this shop on the corner of Fifth Avenue and Milburn Road: the motto of Walter Willson's declares that it is a 'Smiling Service Shop'. (The company was to later drop one of the Ls to become Wilson's). A little girl in a white dress is either trying to post a letter or to peek through the post box slot.

BELSAY – *Italian-style model village, built in the 1840s by Sir Charles Monck*

The old village, which consisted of about eighteen houses, lay to the southwest of Belsay Castle. However, Sir Charles Monck had it demolished and rebuilt further away, near the park gates, in the 1840s. The new village, built in stone and slate, was in fact one long terraced row featuring an arcaded ground floor; this was a reflection of Sir Charles Monck's taste for things Italian. He travelled widely, taking his bride off on a honeymoon that lasted two years, much of it exploring Germany, Italy and Greece. There has been no modern development in the village, which has retained its distinctive character; the village and the adjoining woodland and fields were designated as a Conservation Area in 1987.

Opposite: CULLERCOATS, FISHERMEN'S COTTAGES C1955 C283006

Above: ASHINGTON, MILBURN ROAD C1955 A224022

Right: BELSAY, THE VILLAGE C1955 B554007

Abingdon, Oxfordshire	63	Congleton, Moreton Old Hall, Cheshire	123
Albury, Surrey	44	Corsham, Almshouses, Wiltshire	33
Aldeburgh, The 'Ionia', Suffolk	109	Cranbrook, Kent	54
Alfriston, The Clergy House, Sussex	50	Cropredy, Oxford Canal, Oxfordshire	66
Ambleside, Bridge Cottage, Cumbria	146	Cullercoats, Northumberland	154
Andover, Anton Mill, Hampshire	39	Dorking, Surrey	45
Anna Valley, Hampshire	38	Durham, Co Durham	149, 150
Asfordby, Leicestershire	96	East Dereham, Bishop Bonner's Cottage, Norfolk	114, 115
Ashington, Milburn Road, Northumberland	155	East Horsley, Horsley Towers, Surrey	45
Askrigg, Yorkshire	137	Elstow, Bedfordshire	75
Banbury, Broughton Castle, Oxfordshire	63	Eversley, Charles Kingsley's Rectory, Hampshire	43
Barton Seagrave, Northamptonshire	94	Exmouth, A La Ronde, Devon	19
Bath, Somerset	24-25, 26	Eyam, Derbyshire	129
Belsay, Northumberland	155	Eype, Edith Warren's Teashop, Dorset	29
Bibury, Arlington Row, Gloucestershire	77	Freston Tower, Suffolk	109
Biddestone, Wiltshire	33	Frimley Green, Surrey	47
Blakeney, Norfolk	117	Frome, The Pepper Pot, Somerset	27
Blanchland, Northumberland	151	Galmpton, Devon	14, 15
Bletchingley, Surrey	46	Glastonbury, The Tribunal, Somerset	22
Bodiam Castle, Sussex	54	Grantham, Belvoir Castle, Leicestershire	97
Bolton, Hall i'th the Wood, Greater Manchester	130	Great Yarmouth, The Rows, Norfolk	112
Bonsall, Tufa Cottage, Via Gellia, Derbyshire	128	Grendon Underwood, Buckinghamshire	66
Boscastle, Cornwall	12	Haddon Hall, Derbyshire	126, 127
Bray, Jesus Hospital, Berkshire	60	Harlow, The Round House, Essex	102
Bridgnorth, Cave Dwellings, Shropshire	89	Harpenden, Buckinghamshire	70
Broadway, China Square, Worcestershire	85	Hauxwell, The Rectory, Yorkshire	142
Bromyard, Lower Brockhampton, Herefordshire	83	Hawkshead, Ann Tyson's House, Cumbria	145
Broom, Warwickshire	94	Hawkshead, Flag Street, Cumbria	146
Buckingham, Buckinghamshire	69	Henbury, Blaise Hamlet, Bristol	27
Bucklers Hard, Hampshire	38	Hereford, Herefordshire	81
Burnley, Towneley Hall, Lancashire	132-133	Hertford, Panshanger House, Hertfordshire	71
Buttermere, High Stile, Cumbria	148	Heysham, Cosy Corner, Lancashire	134
Buxton, Derbyshire	125	High Wycombe, Buckinghamshire	67
Camberley, Surrey	47	Higher Bockhampton, Hardy's Birthplace, Dorset	31
Canterbury, Weavers' Cottages, Kent	55	Hingham, Norfolk	115
Castle Combe, Wiltshire	34-35	Hitchin, The Biggin, Hertfordshire	72, 73
Cheltenham, Gloucestershire	78-79	Hope Cove, Devon	16
Chester, Eaton Hall, Cheshire	124	Houghton, Cambridgeshire	118
Chester, Stanley Palace, Cheshire	122	Ickham, Kent	55
Cley-next-the-Sea, Norfolk	117	Ipswich, The Ancient House, Suffolk	107
Cliveden House, Berkshire	61	Jaywick, Essex	105
Clovelly, Devon	20	Kendal, Highgate, Cumbria	143
Cockermouth, Wordsworth's Birthplace, Cumbria	147	Kennington, Kent	55
Compton Wynyates, Warwickshire	92-93	Kersey, Suffolk	108, 109

KNARESBOROUGH, ST ROBERT'S CHAPEL, YORKSHIRE	136
LAYER MARNEY, THE TOWERS, ESSEX	104
LECHLADE, THE ROUND TOWER, GLOUCESTERSHIRE	76
LEDBURY, HEREFORDSHIRE	80
LEOMINSTER, HEREFORDSHIRE	84
LEVENS HALL, CUMBRIA	144-145
LEWES, ANNE OF CLEVES'S HOUSE, SUSSEX	48-49
LINCOLN, JEW'S HOUSE, LINCOLNSHIRE	120-121
LINCOLN, LINCOLNSHIRE	119
LONDON, CHEYNE WALK	55
LONDON, PARK LANE	59
LONDON, NOMADS	59
LUDLOW, THE FEATHERS, SHROPSHIRE	87
LUSTLEIGH, DEVON	13
MAIDS MORETON, BUCKINGHAMSHIRE	69
MAPLEDURHAM MILL, OXFORDSHIRE	64-65
MILTON ABBAS, DORSET	29
MONTACUTE HOUSE, SOMERSET	23
NEWARK, THE GOVERNOR'S HOUSE, NOTTINGHAMSHIRE	99
NEWCASTLE UPON TYNE, THE SANDHILL, NORTHUMBERLAND	152, 153
NEWPORT, CROWN HOUSE, ESSEX	106
NEWQUAY, THE HUER'S HOUSE, CORNWALL	12
NEWSTEAD ABBEY, NOTTINGHAMSHIRE	100
NORTHAMPTON, CASTLE ASHBY, NORTHAMPTONSHIRE	95
NOTTINGHAM, WOLLATON HALL, NOTTINGHAMSHIRE	98
ODIHAM, HAMPSHIRE	43
PADSTOW, PRIDEAUX PLACE, CORNWALL	11
POLPERRO, CORNWALL	8
PORLOCK, THATCHERS, SOMERSET	15
PORTHCURNO, CORNWALL	10
PUDDLETOWN, DORSET	31
QUENIBOROUGH, LEICESTERSHIRE	96
RAMSBURY, WILTSHIRE	37
RICKMANSWORTH, MOOR PARK, HERTFORDSHIRE	71
RINGWOOD, HAMPSHIRE	40-41
RIVINGTON, PIGEON TOWER, LANCASHIRE	131
RYE, SUSSEX	52, 53
ST IVES, CORNWALL	9
ST IVES, OVERCOTE FERRY, CAMBRIDGESHIRE	118
ST MARY'S, ISLE OF SCILLY	10
SAFFRON WALDEN, ESSEX	106
SALHOUSE, NORFOLK	113
SALISBURY, WILTSHIRE	36, 37
SALTAIRE, YORKSHIRE	135
SANDRINGHAM, THE ENTRANCE LODGE, NORFOLK	116
SANDSEND, YORKSHIRE	142
SELBORNE, THE WAKES, HAMPSHIRE	42
SELWORTHY, SOMERSET	21
SIDMOUTH, DEVON	18, 19
SKIPTON, SKIPTON CASTLE, YORKSHIRE	137
SMALLHYTHE, KENT	56-57
SOMERLEYTON HALL, SUFFOLK	110, 111
SONNING, BERKSHIRE	62
SOUTH SHIELDS, LAYGATE LANE, NORTHUMBERLAND	151
SOUTH WEALD, QUEEN MARY'S CHAPEL, ESSEX	102-103
SOUTHWELL, THE BISHOP'S MANOR, NOTTINGHAMSHIRE	101
STOKESAY CASTLE, SHROPSHIRE	88
STOURPORT-ON-SEVERN, CAVE DWELLINGS, WORCESTERSHIRE	84
STRATFORD-UPON-AVON, SHAKESPEARE'S BIRTHPLACE, WARWICKSHIRE	90, 91
THORPENESS, SUFFOLK	110
TIPTREE, MESSING MAYPOLE MILL, ESSEX	103
TORQUAY, DEVON	16, 17
TOTTERNHOE, BEDFORDSHIRE	74
TRING, TRING PARK, HERTFORDSHIRE	71
TURTON TOWER, LANCASHIRE	131
WADDESDON MANOR, BUCKINGHAMSHIRE	68
WEOBLEY, HEREFORDSHIRE	83
WEOBLEY, THE LEY, HEREFORDSHIRE	82
WEST BUCKLAND, DEVON	15
WEYMOUTH, DORSET	28
WHITBY, YORKSHIRE	141
WIMBORNE, DORSET	32
WINCHELSEA, THE ARMOURY, SUSSEX	51
WOKINGHAM, BERKSHIRE	60
WOOL, WOOLBRIDGE MANOR, DORSET	30
WORCESTER, WORCESTERSHIRE	86
WOTTON-UNDER-EDGE, GLOUCESTERSHIRE	76
WROXHAM, BURE COURT, NORFOLK	113
YEOVIL, SOMERSET	22
YORK, YORKSHIRE	138-139, 140

FRANCIS FRITH – Victorian pioneer

FRANCIS FRITH, *founder of the world-famous photographic archive, was a complex and multi-talented man. A devout Quaker and a highly successful Victorian businessman, he was philosophic by nature and pioneering in outlook. By 1855 he had already established a wholesale grocery business in Liverpool, and sold it for the astonishing sum of £200,000, which is the equivalent today of over £15,000,000. Now in his thirties, and captivated by the new science of photography, Frith set out on a series of pioneering journeys up the Nile and to the Near East.*

INTRIGUE AND EXPLORATION

He was the first photographer to venture beyond the sixth cataract of the Nile. Africa was still the mysterious 'Dark Continent', and Stanley and Livingstone's historic meeting was a decade into the future. The conditions for picture taking confound belief. He laboured for hours in his wicker dark-room in the sweltering heat of the desert, while the volatile chemicals fizzed dangerously in their trays. Back in London he exhibited his photographs and was 'rapturously cheered' by members of the Royal Society. His reputation as a photographer was made overnight.

VENTURE OF A LIFE-TIME

By the 1870s the railways had threaded their way across the country, and Bank Holidays and half-day Saturdays had been made obligatory by Act of Parliament. All of a sudden the working man and his family were able to enjoy days out, take holidays, and see a little more of the world.

With typical business acumen, Francis Frith foresaw that these new tourists would enjoy having souvenirs to commemorate their days out. For the next thirty years he travelled the country by train and by pony and trap, producing fine photographs of seaside resorts and beauty spots that were keenly bought by millions of Victorians. These prints were painstakingly pasted into family albums and pored over during the

dark nights of winter, rekindling precious memories of summer excursions. Frith's studio was soon supplying retail shops all over the country, and by 1890 F Frith & Co had become the greatest specialist photographic publishing company in the world, with over 2,000 sales outlets, and pioneered the picture postcard.

FRANCIS FRITH'S LEGACY

Francis Frith died in 1898, his great project still growing. The archive he created continued in business for another seventy years. By 1970 it contained over a third of a million pictures showing 7,000 British towns and villages.

Frith's legacy to us today is of immense significance and value, for the magnificent archive of evocative photographs he created provides a unique record of change in the cities, towns and villages throughout Britain over a century and more. Frith and his fellow studio photographers revisited locations many times down the years to update their views, compiling for us an enthralling and colourful pageant of British life and character.

We are fortunate that Frith was dedicated to recording the minutiae of everyday life. For it is this sheer wealth of visual data, the painstaking chronicle of changes in dress, transport, street layouts, buildings, housing, engineering and landscape that captivates us so much today, offering us a powerful link with the past and with the lives of our ancestors.

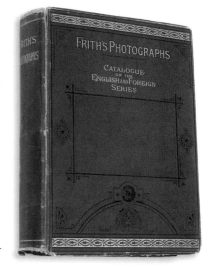

Computers now make Frith's images accessible almost instantly. The archive offers every one of us an opportunity to revisit the places where we and our families have lived and worked down the years. Its images, depicting our shared past, now bring pleasure and enlightenment to many millions, a century after Frith's death.

Oxford, Magdalen College

FREE PRINT OF YOUR CHOICE

Mounted Print
Overall size 14 x 11 inches (355 x 280mm)

CHOOSE A PHOTOGRAPH FROM THIS BOOK

IMPORTANT!

These special prices are only available if you use this form to order.

You must use the ORIGINAL VOUCHER on this page (no copies permitted).

We can only despatch to one UK address.

This offer cannot be combined with any other offer.

Send completed voucher form to:
**The Francis Frith Collection,
Frith's Barn, Teffont, Salisbury,
Wiltshire SP3 5QP**

Choose any Frith photograph in this book.

Simply complete the voucher opposite and return it with your remittance for £3.50 (to cover postage and handling) and we will print the photograph of your choice in SEPIA (size 11 x 8 inches) and supply it in a cream mount with a burgundy rule line (overall size 14 x 11 inches).

Offer valid for delivery to UK addresses only.

PLUS: **Order additional Mounted Prints at HALF PRICE - £7.49 each** (normally £14.99)

If you would like to order more Frith prints from this book, possibly as gifts for friends and family, you can buy them at half price (with no additional postage and handling costs).

PLUS: **Have your Mounted Prints framed**

For an extra £14.95 per print you can have your mounted print(s) framed in an elegant polished wood and gilt moulding, overall size 16 x 13 inches (no additional postage and handling required).

Voucher for *FREE* and Reduced Price *Frith Prints*

Please do not photocopy this voucher. Only the original is valid, so please fill it in, cut it out and return it to us with your order.

Picture ref no	Page no	Qty	Mounted @ £7.49	Framed + £14.95	Total Cost £
		1	Free of charge*	£	£
			£7.49	£	£
			£7.49	£	£
			£7.49	£	£
			£7.49	£	£
			£7.49	£	£

Please allow 28 days for delivery.

Offer available to one UK address only

* Post & handling	£3.50
Total Order Cost	£

Title of this book . . . .

I enclose a cheque/postal order for £ . . . . made payable to 'The Francis Frith Collection'

OR please debit my Mastercard / Visa / Maestro card, details below

Card Number

Issue No (Maestro only)   Valid from (Maestro)

Expires   Signature

Name Mr/Mrs/Ms . . . .

Address . . . .

. . . .

. . . .

. . . . Postcode . . . .

Daytime Tel No . . . .

Email . . . .

Free Print – see overleaf

Can you help us with information about any of the Frith photographs in this book?

We are gradually compiling an historical record for each of the photographs in the Frith archive. It is always fascinating to find out the names of the people shown in the pictures, as well as insights into the shops, buildings and other features depicted.

If you recognize anyone in the photographs in this book, or if you have information not already included in the author's caption, do let us know. We would love to hear from you, and will try to publish it in future books or articles.

Our production team

Frith books are produced by a small dedicated team at offices in the converted Grade II listed 18th-century barn at Teffont near Salisbury, illustrated above. Most have worked with The Francis Frith Collection for many years. All have in common one quality: they have a passion for The Francis Frith Collection. The team is constantly expanding, but currently includes:

Andrew Alsop, Paul Baron, Jason Buck, John Buck, Jenny Coles, Heather Crisp, David Davies, Natalie Davis, Louis du Mont, Isobel Hall, Chris Hardwick, Julian Hight, Peter Horne, James Kinnear, Karen Kinnear, Tina Leary, Stuart Login, Sue Molloy, Sarah Roberts, Kate Rotondetto, Eliza Sackett, Terence Sackett, Sandra Sampson, Adrian Sanders, Sandra Sanger, Julia Skinner, Lewis Taylor, Will Tunnicliffe, David Turner and Ricky Williams.